The Concise Gu
to
Accounting Standards

The Concise Guide to Accounting Standards

Second edition

Roy Dodge FCCA

CHAPMAN AND HALL

University and Professional Division

LONDON • NEW YORK • TOKYO • MELBOURNE • MADRAS

UK   Chapman and Hall, 2–6 Boundary Row, London SE1 8HN

USA   Chapman and Hall, 29 West 35th Street, New York NY10001

JAPAN   Chapman and Hall Japan, Thomson Publishing Japan,
            Hirakawacho Nemoto Building, 7F, 1–7–11 Hirakawa-cho,
            Chiyoda-ku, Tokyo 102

AUSTRALIA   Chapman and Hall Australia, Thomas Nelson Australia,
            480 La Trobe Street, PO Box 4725, Melbourne 3000

INDIA   Chapman and Hall India, R. Seshadri, 32 Second Main
            Road, CIT East, Madras 600 035

First edition 1988
Second edition 1991

© 1988, 1991 R. Dodge

Typeset in 10/11pt Palatino by Columns of Reading
Printed and bound in Great Britain by
T.J. Press (Padstow) Ltd, Padstow, Cornwall

ISBN 0 412 39610 6

British Library Cataloguing in Publication Data
Dodge, Roy
  The concise guide to accounting standards.
  1. Accounting. Standards
  I. Title
  657.0218

  ISBN 0–412–39610–6

Library of Congress Cataloging-in-Publication Data
Dodge, Roy.
  The concise guide to accounting standards / Roy Dodge. —
2nd ed.
    p. cm.
  Includes index.
  ISBN 0–412–39610–6
  1. Accounting—Standards—Great Britain.   I. Title
HF5616.G7D64   1990
657'.021841—dc20   90–2289
                                                        CIP

Contents

Preface

This guide contains a collection of key facts, comments and illustrations on each SSAP.

I originally conceived it as an examination note book for students. As it turned out, the system which I eventually used to catalogue the notes enabled me (or maybe forced me) to produce a more comprehensive book without abandoning my original aim of keeping the work concise. In its final form the guide has many uses.

First it could be used by anyone who wants to find factual information on any SSAP quickly without having to wade through a mass of words in the SSAP itself. This could be the busy practitioner using it as a first source of reference or lecturers and students embroiled in a classroom discussion. The system of cross-referencing, together with the interpretive comments included, should enable users to reach a well informed conclusion on any line of enquiry.

It could certainly be used as a companion guide to the more traditional forms of study text which are popular with students. And there is no reason, except that it is not written in normal text book style, why it should not be used for unaided study. It might take a certain amount of courage and self-reliance to use it this way, but it can be done.

The section called 'Using the Guide' explains how it can be used either as basis for study or for revision. There is also a section at the end called 'Improving Examination Performance'. This is specifically related to answering questions on SSAPs rather than dealing with examination technique in general.

An attempt has been made to analyse each SSAP under seven main headings most of which have a regular system of sub-headings. The nature of certain SSAPs precludes this universal analysis, although a degree of uniformity has been achieved throughout the work. Most headings are self-explanatory and should enable the user to distinguish points of comment and interpretation from those which are factual summary of the SSAP itself.

Comments under the main headings of 'Background' and 'Interesting Points' have, for the most part, been written with a normal sentence structure since the reason for including them was to help students with the discursive aspects of their studies. Those which come under the prescriptive sections such as 'Definitions' and 'The Standard' tend to be in *précis* form and sometimes these will only make sense if read in the context of their own particular sub-heading.

The points summarized under 'Developing the Standard' are mainly based on the explanatory notes to the SSAP. These are particularly important for students since they usually contain a discussion of the concepts as well as a brief outline of the standard being adopted.

The illustrations have been included to give meaning to some of the more ambiguous points in the standard and to help with related areas in accounting practice. Some are very simple. Others deal with complex issues by using simple facts so that the principles can be seen more clearly. Some, particularly those dealing with the more recent SSAPs, may appear to be crammed with detail, but anyone taking the trouble to work through them will soon find that only the essentials have been included.

Apart from the notes and illustrations the book contains various sections which students may find useful. There is a commentary on the general state of the SSAP programme, an SSAP overview which provides a summary of the key points in each SSAP, some examples of accounting policies from published accounts and a table showing the state of harmonization between SSAPs and IASs.

In view of the renewed interest being shown by examiners in accounting for the effects of inflation, notes on the defunct SSAP 16 have been retained. I have also provided an additional commentary on inflation accounting in Appendix 3. This includes an illustrated comparison between HCA, CCA, CPP, and Real Terms accounting.

Abbreviations and references

An attempt has been made to avoid using too many abbreviations. Those which are used are either so much a part of the accountant's everyday language as to be widely understood or their full meaning was introduced earlier in the relevant text. The following are included:

ACT   — Advance corporation tax
ASB   — Accounting Standards Board
ASC   — Accounting Standards Committee
ASSC — Accounting Standards Steering Committee
CA   — Companies Act
CCA   — Current cost accounting (or accounts)
DTI   — Department of Trade and Industry
ED   — Exposure draft
HCA   — Historic cost accounting (or accounts)
IAS   — International Accounting Standard
ICAEW — Institute of Chartered Accountants in England and Wales
Sch. — Schedule
Sec. — Section

At the time of putting the finishing touches to this second edition, the work of the ASC was being transferred to the new Accounting Standards Board (ASB). It should be obvious from the context in which the abbreviation ASC has been used, as to whether such reference should be construed as relating to the new ASB.

The impact of SSAPs on examinations

One of the difficulties facing the present generation of accountancy students is how to cope with the growing maze of accounting regulations and official pronouncements which provide a constant flow of material for the examiners.

Foremost amongst these regulations are the Statements of Standard Accounting Practice issued by the Accounting Standards Committee. Each additional SSAP not only creates a new and separable topic of its own but usually has connecting links with other regulations, concepts and working rules. At the time of writing this first edition there have been twenty-four standards issued over the course of twenty years. Two of these (SSAPs 7 and 11) were aborted shortly after their publication and one (SSAP 16) has been withdrawn although it remains 'an authoritative reference on accounting under the current cost convention'.

There is some comfort in knowing that the proliferation of accounting standards in the UK has not taken on anything like the proportions found in the USA. Furthermore we seem to have reached a point where the initial surge of issues in UK has died down and future growth in SSAPs will be slow. The ASC have indicated that the majority of future pronouncements are likely to be in the form of Statements of Recommended Practice (SORPs) and revisions to existing standards.

Even so, there is already a substantial bulk for students to contend with and I cannot understand why examiners in the professional bodies have not yet mooted the idea of letting students take the actual SSAPs into the examination room. Questions which require a student to do little more than restate the contents of an SSAP are not really a test of ability. The accountant in practice has access to the SSAPs, and he does not usually refer to them so that he can tell someone what they say; he is probably solving a problem, and this is what students should be learning to do.

At the moment questions on SSAPs come in various forms including the application of principles to particular problems. One common factor is that the student will not get very far without learning and being able to recall the essential contents of the SSAP. But this is only a start. Examiners frequently expect students to be able to discuss critically a whole network of related matters. The possibility that students are having difficulty with this can be detected from an analysis of past questions and results for the examination paper 'The Regulatory Framework of Accounting' set by The Chartered Association of Certified Accountants.

The new syllabus for these examinations started in June 1982 and by June 1986 there had been 54 questions set with 24 (45%) having a direct reference to SSAPs. Some of the remaining questions related indirectly to the problem of accounting standards. It would be wrong for students to assume from my analysis that the examiner has abused the published weightings (25% for the institutional framework) since I have based it on 6 questions per paper and only 5 have to be answered. Furthermore some of the questions are hybrids which makes it difficult to classify them distinctly.

Published pass rates for this paper in recent years show it to be amongst the most difficult to pass in Level 2. In 1985 it took bottom place with a pass rate of 27%. In 1984 and 1986, with a pass rate of 32% in both years, it came within one percentage point of being at the bottom of the table.

There are probably many factors which contribute to this, but included amongst them must be the sheer volume of material which the student is expected to absorb during study and then recall during the exam. The chances are that a fair proportion of what was understood during the study will not be retained for very long. It is all too easy, even amongst those of us who try to write textbooks on the subject, to feel like one of my students who said: 'One day I know it, the next day I don't.'

It was partly on this premise that I decided to write this book. It was originally intended to be a guide to be read during the revision period. The SSAPs themselves, or even an exposition of them in a study text, will present the student with far too much verbiage to wade through during those hectic and panic-stricken hours. On the other hand some study texts are so short on detail that the student is left poorly informed.

As the book evolved it became obvious to me that it could also be used as a source of reference in the course of normal study. The next section, called 'Using the Guide', has been written to help students who intend to use it in that way.

Using the guide

There are various ways in which the guide could be used in preparing for exams. No doubt some students who buy it will adopt their own (or tutor's) ideas but I would like to give my advice to the struggling majority of professional students who have no access to tutorial guidance and have to rely on their own endeavours.

There are two important points to think about:

1) the order in which the book is used in relation to any other sources of study material you may have;
2) the order in which you study the SSAPs.

Order of use with other sources

Having decided which SSAP to study (see below) you should first refer to the relevant notes in the section called 'SSAP overview'. The notes given are not very detailed but they do give a broad idea of the contents of each SSAP, and will provide a key for the detailed study.

Next read through the notes in the guide. This will at least provide a key to what you need to know. It may be presumptive to suggest it, but I believe a fair number of notes can be understood without reference to other sources. If any do not convey a satisfactory meaning, then use them as a prompt to explore your own sources. Do not make your own notes in the book at this stage (use rough paper) since you may eventually find they are unnecessary.

If parts of the study are difficult to understand there is no reason why you should not skip over these and return to them later. Skipping points does not usually stop you from understanding those which follow, and quite often when you go back to the item you skipped it does not seem so difficult after all.

Once satisfied with the core of your study, read through the notes in the guide again. Don't worry if you cannot understand everything, particularly things like the definitions used in SSAP 21. These should become clear as you work through the examples, the next stage.

Work through the examples if you did not do so in the course of your study.

Read through the overview again and make any additional notes of your own on the blank pages provided. Don't be afraid to keep them very short. Students tend to make their notes too long because they think it will help them to remember how points were explained in the text. It is the point you need to remember, now how someone else explained it (you are likely to forget that anyway).

Make a note on the control sheet (page xl) that you have studied the SSAP.

You should constantly review material previously studied in order to keep your recall ability at its highest peak. Students are notoriously bad at doing this, probably because they think that having understood something they will be able to recall it later. But it is very easy to forget ('One day I know it, the next day I don't'), particularly when there is so much to absorb. The notes in the guide should form the basis of these reviews, the first of which needs to be about two days after completing the study.

During your planned pre-exam revision period it should only be necessary to read through the notes in the guide. On your way to the exam hall you should not be reading anything, but undoubtedly you will want to. If you cannot control the urge then I suggest you simply read through the notes in the overview. If these should set up some kind of panic you can turn to the more detailed notes in the guide. If that fails to calm you down, try deep breathing or thinking about your most recent pleasurable experience; you should be able to remember that!

SSAP groupings

The most logical sequence for presenting material in the guide was thought to be SSAP number order. Unfortunately this is not the most logical sequence for study of the SSAPs themselves.

With 21 operative standards issued over the course of 20 years there is bound to be interaction between some which make it desirable to use groupings as a basis for study. Furthermore, as critics are quick to point out, there are inconsistencies between certain standards and these can enliven a subject which might otherwise seem dull

Authors of textbooks and manuals usually adopt their own method of grouping SSAPs together for presentation of their text. Where you are using such material as your primary source of study I need hardly say any more. The order of study has been determined for you.

Some students may already have read the classification of SSAPs made by Professor H.C. Edey and published in *Studies of Accounting* (3rd edition). I am not going to suggest that his analysis is used as a basis for dividing the subject into study segments because that was not its objective. However, it does tend to influence a choice of order and is interesting enough in its own right.

Professor Edey pointed out that SSAPs were basically dealing with four questions which need to be considered when financial statements are being prepared. He gave them 'type' numbers which can be summarized as follows:

Type 1 Description. What principles have been used?
Type 2 Presentation. How should certain items be presented?
Type 3 Disclosure. What information needs to be disclosed?
Type 4 Valuation and profit measurement. What method is recommended in particular circumstances for measurement of items affecting profit and the carrying values of assets and liabilities?

The sequence of type numbers does not follow the sequence of thought processes which usually occur when accounts are prepared. This is more likely to be type 4 first followed by types 1 2 and 3.

Types 1 to 3 attract very little controversy. In fact most of their provisions have now been written into company accounting legislation. Type 1 was originally SSAP 2 but each subsequent SSAP which allowed a choice on a type 4 problem made its own provisions for disclosure of the policy adopted. Standards dealing with type 4 questions are the most controversial and provide a constant source of material for debate.

The network of connecting links between SSAPs is now such that attempts to chart a path through it is almost bound to lead to a loose end somewhere. I have therefore included a section in each guide called 'cross-references'. These are not meant to be complete since I have only mentioned those which I thought would be more fruitful. The more obvious have been omitted. You should not ignore these interconnections. One common weakness I have noticed in students' answers is that they tend to limit their discussion to provisions of the SSAP named or implied by the question.

International standards are mentioned in the 'cross-references' section together with comments on points of difference if there are any worth noting.

As a plan for study my preferred groupings and sequence of SSAPs within each group are set out in the following table. The title of each group does not give a precise description of matters dealt with by the SSAPs listed – many cannot be sorted into such categories. SSAP 12 for example is related more to accounting measurements than basic principles, SSAP 10 is usually dealt with under presentation but will be more helpful to students if read in connection with group accounting. The sequence in each category is deliberate and includes a consideration of how learning points will be accumulated by working through the examples in this guide.

Group	*Sequence of study*
Basic concepts:	SSAP 2, SSAP 12
Presentation:	SSAP 6, SSAP 8, SSAP 3, SSAP 15, SSAP 5
Group accounting:	SSAP 14, SSAP 1, SSAP 22, SSAP 10, SSAP 23, SSAP 20
Accounting measurements:	SSAP 17 and 18, SSAP 4, SSAP 9, SSAP 13, SSAP 19, SSAP 21, SSAP 24
Special concepts:	SSAP 16, Appendix 3

A change of policy

The purpose of this section is simply to make some comment on the current state of the SSAP programme. It is written to stimulate general interest; my cavalier style is not likely to attract the attention of any examiner let alone those who set the standards.

Achievement

The events leading up to public doubts over the credibility of the accounting profession and the formation of the Accounting Standards Committee are now well documented. I imagine most students using this work are likely to have studied them previously. Now that the initial flurry of pronouncements has died down and having reviewed all existing SSAPs to produce this guide it seemed like a good moment to take stock of achievements so far and comment on possible future developments.

In general terms the SSAP programme has been accepted by members of the profession and the interested public as a means of self-regulation. But it is not without its critics. The most frequent criticism which students read about is the lack of a conceptual framework. We have not, so the thesis goes, defined profit nor properly identified users' needs and it is the lack of such a framework which has not only made so many standards necessary but allowed inconsistencies to creep in between some of them.

The arguments in this respect may all be plausible but as a body of practical men accountants cannot sit back and wait for a conceptual framework. The publication of audited financial statements each year will have to go on unless someone can find a better way of instilling financial discipline into economic activity. Business itself will never be static and new situations are bound to arise which will be the subject of different accounting interpretations.

The pragmatic piecemeal approach to standard setting which the ASC embarked upon was the only one possible in the circumstances. It is characterized by SSAP 1 being on a particular practical problem whereas the first standard to deal with any kind of conceptual matter was relegated to SSAP 2. This piecemeal process has been going on over the course of 20 years and so it is hardly surprising that inconsistencies can be found between different standards.

Review

When a standard is issued the ASC do not have the benefit of hindsight which their critics eventually have and they are dealing with something which is constantly moving. The SSAP programme therefore includes a system of periodic reviews and amendments. Perhaps the time has now come for someone to tidy up the whole package of existing SSAPs before any more are added or amended. If urgent problems arise in the meantime a temporary solution could be found through the programme of SORPs which the ASC indicate are likely to form the core of future announcements.

Leaving aside any conflicts of principle, my review of all SSAPs shows a noticeable inconsistency in presentation. Some earlier standards seem to include definitions or other important matters in the explanatory notes which are not always covered by the prescriptive part of the SSAP. By contrast some later SSAPs repeat definitions which are common to more than one standard, such as: company, financial statements, equity share capital, and fair value.

Furthermore, as might have been anticipated, the SSAP programme has unearthed more concepts than we thought we had when we started. Some of them seem to get lost on the route between discussion and standard but we now talk about the articulation concept (related to consistency) when discussing SSAP 12, the 'all-inclusive concept of profit' (in contrast to current operating concept) in SSAP 6 and the capital maintenance concept as a result of SSAP 16.

Reorganize

It should be possible to reorganize the standards so that the first becomes a basket for any concepts, definitions and rules of practical application, which might apply to standards generally. It could be fuelled by research and amended from time to time. It may even become the elusive conceptual framework. It is worth pointing out that some of the earliest work on standards in America (1939) related to definitions.

Then there are areas where SSAPs could be consolidated. Group accounts is a good example (an unfortunate clash of words!) and presumably the ASB will do this now that the EC 7th Directive has been incorporated into UK law by the 1989 Companies Act. When SSAP 14 was first rushed out most of us thought that it referred to acquisition accounting because that was what we had learned to do over the years. Relatively few practitioners had heard of pooling, let alone used it in practice. By the time SSAP 23 came out we realized that SSAP 14 did not, except to a limited extent, refer to acquisition accounting at all.

SSAP 23 deals with both acquisition and merger accounting for groups. There is no reason to leave some of the regulations in SSAP 14 or, for that matter, in SSAP 1.

Definitions

As regards definitions I think it is a pity that the standards sometimes simply repeat those found in legislation. SSAP 14 is a good example because the definitions of subsidiary and equity share capital are taken from the Companies Act (prior to the 1989 amendments).

Anyone reading the legal definition of equity share capital could easily think it is actually defining preference share capital. Perhaps the legal draughtsman was trying to avoid the word 'only' and in doing so has resorted to a kind of double negative. (Trying to spot a badly used 'only' in official prose was a popular sport at one time because of the way it created ambiguities if placed in the wrong part of the sentence.) Perhaps the ASC decided that a legal definition should not be tampered with. If that was so we should think about it again. Accountancy is nothing if it does not communicate and an example could be set by using plain language for our own domestic regulations, even at the risk of losing a little precision.

Concepts

On the question of concepts we seem to be waiting for the conceptual framework to put this house in order. In the meantime it would be helpful if some official effort were made to improve the language. It is probably a low priority since it tends to be academic rather than practical. But at the moment we (authors and so on) are all relatively free to use words like concepts, principles, and assumptions (even words which sound more intellectual such as postulates and axioms!) as if they were all interchangeable. We even get them mixed up with common-sense working rules like 'materiality' and 'substance over form'. This can be a pitfall for students.

A good exercise for anyone embarking on a study of accounting standards is to make a comparison between SSAP 2 and IAS 1 as regards basic concepts, assumptions and working rules. It may not make you any better at preparing accounts when your time comes but it could make you more careful when answering exam questions.

I remember a recent exam question where students were asked to discuss the concepts in SSAP 21 (leases and hire purchase). I used this question in a mock exam and most students eloquently described the idea of 'substance over form'. No doubt many of the students taking the real exam did the same thing, yet apparently the examiner was looking for 'investment period principle'.

Accountants have talked about 'substance over form' for many years particularly in relation to hire purchase. It first seems to have received official recognition in IAS 1 but it does not qualify as a concept and is not mentioned in either SSAP 2 or SSAP 21. Concepts always seem to be endowed with higher intellectual qualities than working rules and this may partly explain the reluctance to tinker with them.

Change of accounting policy

The practical application of concepts is achieved by adopting accounting policies. When companies change the way in which certain items are treated the accountant has to consider whether the change is a change of accounting policy. The importance of this relates to adjustments of brought forward figures. Where the change qualifies as a change of policy such adjustments can be treated as a prior year adjustment under SSAP 6.

Recent developments show this to be less straightforward than one would expect. Most of us would have thought that a change of method in calculating depreciation was a change of policy but it has now been pointed out in the revised SSAP 12 that this is not so. It does not explain why and to find an answer to this we have to look for clues embedded in SSAP 2 and the revised SSAP 6.

We are told by the new SSAP 6 that a change of policy can only arise as a result of a choice between two or more accounting bases. Bases, according to SSAP 2, are the practical methods developed for applying fundamental concepts. In the case of fixed asset costs the fundamental concept which has to be applied is accruals, and the method developed to apply that concept is depreciation under SSAP 12.

It seems that in the case of fixed asset costs (save for the exceptions stated in SSAP 12) we have no choice of base and therefore no choice of policy at all. If we change the way depreciation is calculated we have simply modified the policy.

I am not entirely sure whether my reasoning on this is in keeping with the official view, because that has not been set out clearly in the SSAPs concerned. It sounds convincing up to a point but then I am left puzzled by the definition of bases in SSAP 2 where it refers to 'methods' developed for applying fundamental concepts. Surely straight line and reducing balance are methods developed!

The point is that it should not have been necessary for me to try to make sense of such a basic point by searching in this way. Enough work has now been done to enable such matters to be codified in my suggested SSAP on concepts, definitions and rules of practical application.

If the existing SSAP 1 could be incorporated into any new standard on groups where it really belongs it would leave that number free to be used as suggested. The existing SSAP 2 has to a large extent become redundant since most problems envisaged at the time have been covered in subsequent SSAPs.

Attitudes

Finally, as some accountants seem to thrive on interpreting the rules, we could take a look to see if the rules themselves have had any influence on professional attitudes.

We are told that before we had standards we had too much freedom over how we were allowed to interpret the generally accepted accounting principles. We could not be trusted to apply them fairly and some events proved that to be so. Being amongst the practising accountants at the time I know that we often considered alternatives in the light of trying to keep everyone happy. Somehow we convinced ourselves that we were being fair.

Have standards made that much difference? They have certainly created a healthy debate and have tried to provide the delicate balance between freedom and order. But we still have discussions, both public and private, which seem to play on how far we can bend the rules and yet remain fair. For example, all the energy spent on debating 'split depreciation' in the professional press (until the new SSAP 12 ruled it out) was mostly concerned with whether or not the idea was legal. We conducted the discussion as if we were analysing a piece of tax legislation in order to establish a legitimate way of avoiding tax. We gave very little thought to the spirit or the concepts, perhaps we only do that when it suits us.

Practising accountants know that financial accounting has always been sufficiently malleable to allow some creativity, no doubt this will continue despite valiant attempts by the ASC, or any other body taking over the standard setting process. In recent times, much attention has been focused on the creative accounting opportunities provided by business combinations. Excessive provisions (blamed on poor management of the victim company) are created in the victim company's books, and then fed back into post-acquisition profits in order to show how successful the new management has been.

And accounting is not only creative in being able to manipulate profits between accounting periods, we can even create a new language. If writing off goodwill leaves a gaping hole in the balance sheet, we create another asset ('Brands') to take its place because we worry about giving the wrong impression of what the business is worth. But are balance sheets really meant to contain information on what a business is worth? If they are, then we must find another way of doing them.

Sources and acknowledgments

My principal sources were the SSAPs EDs and IASs and a publication by Deloitte Haskins and Sells called *Accounting Provisions of the Companies Act 1985* written by Barry Johnson FCA and Matthew Patient FCA. The title of their book is little misleading since it includes a wealth of helpful information on accounting standards. I was also influenced to some extent by the writings of Mike Harvey and Fred Keer in their book *Financial Accounting Theory* published by Prentice Hall International.

Many of the original draft notes and illustrations were field tested on a group of student accountants in Deloittes of Zambia and I wish to thank them for the various ways in which they helped me to shape the final product.

I am most grateful to the members of Van Nostrand Reinhold's review panel who made many useful suggestions and pointed out various omissions. I have not been able to incorporate every suggestion they made for if I had done so the book would have been far too voluminous for those whose benefit it is intended.

I am also grateful to Stephen Wellings, my sponsoring editor, who I am sure sensed my occasional moods of despair and managed to say just the right thing to keep me going.

SSAP overview

The official published text of 21 SSAPs (24 issued, 3 withdrawn) and their related guidelines, covers some 286 pages of very small print. It is not possible, therefore, to give anything other than a broad overview in the following notes. Further details of each SSAP will be obtained by working through the notes and illustrations in the main section of the guide.

Background

The objective of accounting standards can be stated as:

1) to assist in the exercise of judgement, e.g. by issuing explanatory notes and guidelines;
2) to reduce the number of acceptable practices;
3) to improve the information content of published financial statements, and improve their comparability.

The explanatory forward to all SSAPs implies that accounting standards should be applied to 'all financial statements whose purpose is to give a true and fair view'. This idea of universality has been eroded by several subsequent SSAPs and a variety of exemptions, based on different criteria, now apply.

Some exemptions are based on specified limits (SSAP 10 on turnover), some on the type of industry (SSAPs 12 and 19), some on whether or not the company is listed (SSAP 3 and previously SSAP 16). The ASC have also been considering additional exemption criteria that could apply to future SSAPs. These may include a distinction between public and private companies, and exemptions for companies classified by the Companies Act as small, or medium-sized.

This hotchpotch of exemptions could make it difficult for users of accounts to draw reasonable conclusions, and make comparisons, since they will not always know which standards applied to the companies concerned.

Summary of key points

The following summary is divided between SSAPs of general interest, and those relating to group accounts.

SSAP 1 ASSOCIATED COMPANIES

See section on Group Accounts.

SSAP 2 DISCLOSURE OF ACCOUNTING POLICIES

Accounting policies adopted must be disclosed.

The four fundamental concepts of: going concern, accruals, consistency, and prudence are presumed to have been observed unless there is a clear statement otherwise (e.g. statement that an accounting policy has been changed).

Where a company has a choice of accounting bases (methods developed to apply the fundamental concepts) the one chosen becomes the company's accounting policy. It should be applied consistently (fundamental concept) and disclosed in notes to the financial statements.

SSAP 3 EARNINGS PER SHARE

Listed companies must disclose earnings per share (EPS) for the current and previous periods. The earnings per share is used by investment analysts in the price earnings (P/E) ratio (e.g. as published by the Financial Times in their share price listings).

Earnings are basically 'ordinary profits' available for distribution to ordinary shareholders (i.e. extraordinary items are excluded). Earnings per share will therefore be: consolidated profit after tax, minority interests, and preference dividends but before extraordinary items; divided by the number of ordinary shares in issue and ranking for dividend.

When new shares have been issued during the current period it may be necessary to adjust EPS of the previous year for comparative purposes (the trend in P/E ratios is important to investment analysts). A bonus issue is treated as if the shares had been in issue throughout the whole of the current and previous year. An issue at full market price will only affect earning potential from the date of issue and therefore the current year's earnings are divided by the weighted number of shares in issue during the year – no adjustment is needed to previous year's EPS. A rights issue is treated as partly a bonus issue and partly an issue at full market price – the bonus element involves making an adjustment to EPS for the previous year.

The effect of the bonus element in a rights issue can be dealt with by using the formula suggested in the SSAP, as follows:

EPS for previous year is multiplied by the fraction:

$$\frac{\text{theoretical ex rights price}}{\text{actual cum rights price}}$$

For the current year, the weighted average number of shares in issue prior to the rights issue is multiplied by the inverse of this fraction and the result is added to the weighted average in issue after the rights issue.

Diluted earnings per share applies where the company has capital in issue which can be converted into equity at some future time, e.g. convertible debentures (or preference shares) and share options.

Diluted EPS is calculated for the current year on the basis of what it would be if the maximum number of options had been exercised at the beginning of the period (or date stock issued if later). This may involve adjustments to earnings for items such as interest (or preference dividends) which would no longer be payable if the options were exercised. In the case of share options it is necessary to increase earnings by a notional income based on the amount of interest (net of corporation tax) that would be received if the subscription proceeds were invested in 2½ % Consolidated Stock at the beginning of the period (or date the options were issued if later).

SSAP 4 GOVERNMENT GRANTS

Capital based grants must be capitalized and amortized to profit over the expected useful life of the asset. At present, this can be achieved in one of two ways:

1) By crediting grant to cost of asset and depreciating reduced figure.
2) By crediting grant to a separate deferred credit account whereby the gross asset cost is depreciated and the deferred credit amortized at the same rate as depreciation.

As a result of ED43, this choice of method may be removed and standard practice will be restricted to be the deferred credit basis.

SSAP 5 VALUE ADDED TAX

Turnover not to include VAT; creditors (or debtors) for VAT need not be disclosed separately.

SSAP 6 EXTRAORDINARY ITEMS AND PRIOR YEAR ADJUSTMENTS

All items should pass through the profit and loss account except where law or accounting standards permit (or require) otherwise. This is the 'all inclusive concept' of profit. Unusual items may be 'exceptional' if they result from ordinary activities or 'extraordinary' if they arise from events outside of ordinary activities. Profits and losses resulting from terminated activities are examples of extraordinary items.

Most profits or losses on the sale of fixed assets fall to be classified as ordinary since they are likely to be part of an asset replacement policy – sometimes it may be appropriate to treat them as 'exceptional' e.g. if the amounts are material and do not occur frequently. They would be extraordinary if they arose from the termination of a business segment.

Prior year adjustments must not include normal adjustments to previous accounting estimates (e.g. taxation provisions), and only apply to adjustments which result from a change of accounting policy or from a fundamental error. A change of method for calculating depreciation is not a change of policy – simply a modification to an existing one.

SSAP 8 TAXATION

Dividends received must be presented as part of the ordinary profit before tax as 'franked investment income' i.e. cash amount received plus the related tax credit. The tax credit is then treated as a component of the tax charge.

Payment of ACT (following payment of a dividend) is dealt with under the accruals concept. The full amount of taxation on the profits for the year is expensed and ACT is treated as a payment on account of the amount owing (i.e reduces the liability) in the same way as payment to any other creditor. ACT will not, therefore, be seen as an item in the profit and loss account unless (in very exceptional circumstances) it is considered unrecoverable – in which case it must be written off as part of the tax charge.

ACT which will become payable in the next year, as a result of paying any dividends proposed for the current year, must be provided in the current year's balance sheet: credit ACT payable (creditor falling due within one year) and debit ACT recoverable. The ACT recoverable should be set off against the deferred tax account, or shown as a deferred asset if there is no deferred tax account.

SSAP 9 STOCKS AND WORK IN PROGRESS

Stocks to be valued as the aggregate of the lower of cost or net realizable value (NRV) of the separate items of stock. Cost is all expenditure in the normal course of business in bringing stock to its existing state and location.

Cost of stocks manufactured by the company must include fixed production overheads absorbed on the basis of normal capacity.

NRV means estimated (or known) selling price, less costs of completion, marketing and distribution. Replacement price is not normally applicable unless it gives an indication of NRV.

Identifying costs requires the exercise of judgement over the choice of method. The method selected by management must give the fairest practicable approximation to actual expenditure. LIFO and Base Stock methods do not normally do this. Standard cost is acceptable providing it bears a reasonable approximation to 'actual costs' for the period (i.e. standards are regularly reviewed and revised).

The valuation of work in progress for long-term contracts (i.e. those where the time taken to complete the contract falls into different accounting periods) is subject to additional rules.

Where the outcome of the contract can be foreseen, a proportion of the eventual profit which fairly reflects profit attributable to the work performed to date, must be credited to profit and loss. This is achieved by recording turnover earned to date and by transferring a related proportion of the contract costs to cost of sales.

The whole of a foreseeable loss must be written off (credit contract costs, debit profit and loss account).

Progress payments are treated as payments on account of turnover. If the cumulative turnover recognised to date exceeds payments on account, the excess represents 'amounts recoverable on contracts' and is separately disclosed within debtors. If payments on account are greater than turnover to date, the excess is deducted from the balance of costs (i.e. the balance not yet transferred to profit as cost of sales) on the contract – any excess over such costs being classified with creditors.

SSAP 10 SOURCE AND APPLICATION OF FUNDS

The SSAP contains very little by way of prescription other than to require that a funds statement is presented (there is no statutory requirement to do so). There are some requirements regarding presentation and disclosure and most of these can be satisfied by using formats suggested in the Appendix to SSAP 10.

The requirement to present a funds statement is justified on the grounds that the profit and loss account by itself does not provide a sufficient link between the opening and closing balances for a full understanding of changes in the financial position. The funds statement helps to identify such movements by summarizing and re-classifying information from the statutory financial statements.

Contents of statement: operating profit and adjustments for items not involving movement of funds; dividends paid; fixed assets acquired and disposed; cash flows through changes in loan capital (long and medium term) and issued capital; increases and decreases in working capital sub-divided into its component parts; and movements in net liquid funds.

The only item defined by the SSAP is 'net liquid funds', defined as cash, cash equivalents (e.g. current asset investments) less overdrafts and borrowings repayable within one year.

The word 'funds' is not defined and is used in a working capital (accruals) context so that funds from profit can be linked through the other cash movements to changes in working capital.

Guidance on contents: minimum of netting off; figures generally identifiable with those in the profit and loss account and balance sheet. See section on group accounts for further notes on SSAP 10.

SSAP 12 DEPRECIATION

All assets with a finite life must be depreciated. Depreciation results from a reduction in economic life of an asset and must be provided so as to allocate cost (or revalued amount) less residual value, to periods expected to benefit from its use.

Depreciation charged against profits must be based on the carrying value of the asset (i.e. cost or revalued amount). A change of method is not a change of policy. If asset lives are revised it is normal to write off the net book value over the revised remaining useful economic life (i.e no prior year adjustment is normally required).

SSAP 13 RESEARCH AND DEVELOPMENT COSTS

All research costs must be written off as incurred. Development costs may be deferred if certain criteria are satisfied, namely:

1) clearly defined project;
2) expenditure separately identifiable;
3) outcome assessed with reasonable certainty as to technical feasibility and commercial viability;
4) future revenues are reasonably expected to cover aggregate of all development costs on project;
5) adequate resources exist to complete the project.

A possible mnemonic for the above is 'DIARCO' standing for Defined, Identifiable, Assessed, Revenues, COmplete.

The cost of research and development undertaken for third parties may be treated as work in progress until reimbursed.

Deferred development costs should be amortized systematically as soon as commercial production commences. Where the circumstances which justified deferral are no longer applicable, the unamortized expenditure must be written off immediately. Expenditure written off cannot be reinstated.

SSAP 14 GROUP ACCOUNTS

See section on group accounts.

SSAP 15 DEFERRED TAX

Deferred tax should only be provided for timing differences which are expected to crystalize into liabilities (or assets). Calculation of the amount provided should be based on the liability method i.e at the tax rate expected to apply on reversal of the timing difference. Latest tax rates can be used unless future rates are known; adjustments to the outstanding balance will be required if the tax rates change.

The most common timing difference relates to fixed asset costs which are written off in different periods as between accounting profit (depreciation) and taxable profit (capital allowances). Other timing differences include:

1) deferred development costs (allowed for tax as paid, amortized in accounts);
2) interest paid and received (accruals in accounts, cash basis for tax);
3) revaluations (not taxable until sold);
4) trading losses carried forward (relieved when profits are available);
5) pension costs (allowed for tax as paid, cost spreading in accounts).

The combined effect of all timing differences (not individual items) should be considered in deciding whether liabilities are likely to crystallize. The most common situation where a hard core of originating timing differences can create a permanent deferral is where a company is constantly investing in new plant and machinery.

SSAP 16 CURRENT COST ACCOUNTING

Now withdrawn. Note that the 'Alternative Accounting Rules' in the Companies Act permit CCA accounts to be published as the main financial statements, and also permit HCA accounts to be modified by the revaluation of certain assets.

SSAP 17 POST BALANCE SHEET EVENTS

Post balance sheet events are those which occur between the balance sheet date and the date when the financial statements are signed by the directors. They will either be:

1) adjusting events,
2) non-adjusting events.

Adjusting events: post balance sheet events which provide additional evidence of conditions existing at the balance sheet date, e.g. a debt considered to be recoverable at the balance sheet date may have to be written off if, during the post balance sheet period, notification is received that the debtor has become insolvent.

Non-adjusting events: post balance sheet events which relate to conditions that arose subsequent to the balance sheet date, e.g. destruction of a fixed asset through some catastrophe. Where material, such events require disclosure. They would only involve adjustment to the figures if they were of such magnitude as to negate the application of the going concern concept.

SSAP 18 CONTINGENT GAINS AND LOSSES

A contingency is a condition existing at the balance sheet date where the outcome will be confirmed by the occurrence (or non occurrence) of an uncertain future event. A contingent gain or loss is one dependant upon that contingency e.g. there is a contingent loss if the company is defending a court case in respect of a claim for damages relating to an alleged act of negligence – the loss is contingent upon losing the case.

Material contingent losses should be accrued if it is 'probable' that the future event will confirm the loss and the amount can be estimated with reasonable accuracy. If not accrued because of uncertainties it should be disclosed in the notes unless the possibility of a loss is 'remote'.

Material contingent gains should not be accrued. They should only be disclosed in the notes if it is 'probable' the the gain will be realized. If it is 'reasonably certain' that a gain will be realized, such gain is not contingent and would be recognised in the accounts under the normal accruals concept.

SSAP 19 INVESTMENT PROPERTIES

Investment properties are not held for consumption in the course of business but as investments, the disposal of which would result in a re-investment of the funds and have no material affect on trading operations. Therefore, current value and changes in that value are more relevant than depreciation.

Investment properties are those held as investment for rental income negotiated at arm's length. Such properties (other than leaseholds with an unexpired term of 20 years or less) are exempt from the provisions of SSAP 12.

Changes in value are not taken to profit and loss but are shown as movements on an investment revaluation reserve. Excess deficits on this reserve must be written off to profit and loss.

SSAP 20 FOREIGN CURRENCY TRANSLATION

Notes regarding the translation of foreign branches and subsidiaries are included in the section dealing with group accounts. The following notes deal with overseas transactions which can be entered into by any company (whether they have an overseas subsidiary or not) such as sales, purchases, investment, and borrowing.

Transactions (e.g. a purchase of a fixed asset from overseas) should be recorded at the rate of exchange applying when incurred. Thereafter non-monetary assets (e.g. a fixed asset) should be carried at the translated amount. Monetary items outstanding at the balance sheet date (e.g. the amount owing) should be translated at the closing rate.

Gains or losses on settled transactions, and on unsettled short-term monetary items (e.g. the amount owing) are, or soon will be, reflected in cash flows and should be credited to profit and loss account.

Long-term monetary items (e.g. money borrowed from overseas) should be translated to the closing rate each year (unless the rate on maturity is known) and gains or losses should be recognised in the profit and loss account under the accruals concept.

SSAP 21 LEASES AND HIRE PURCHASE

Leases are classified as either finance leases or operating leases.

Finance lease: the lessee agrees to make payments to lessor which will cover the lessor's cost of the asset together with a return on finance provided. Defined as one that transfers substantially all the risks and rewards of ownership (other than legal title) to the lessee. Such transfer presumed if, at inception, the present value of minimum lease payments is substantially all (normally 90% or more) of the fair value of the asset.

Hire purchase: contracts have characteristics similar to finance leases. The main difference is that under hire purchase, the hirer is normally given an option to purchase the asset at the end of the lease term. This will not happen with the usual form of finance lease because in order for the lessor to obtain capital allowances (and lessee to charge rentals as an expense for tax) the lessor is not allowed to sell the residue to the lessee. In most finance leases there is either a secondary term at a nominal rental, or the asset is sold to a third party and a proportion of the sale proceeds (e.g. 95 to 97%) are given to the lessee as a rental rebate.

The lessee: of a finance lease should capitalize the asset, and obligation on inception, at the present value of minimum lease payments. In practice the 'fair value' of the asset will be sufficiently close and may be used. Rentals paid should be apportioned between a reduction of the obligation, and a finance charge, so as to give a constant periodic rate of charge on the amount outstanding. Apportionments may be calculated on either, an actuarial basis, or by using the sum of digits method.

The lessor: must record the transaction as a sale and show the 'net investment in the lease' as a debtor. Gross earnings are allocated to accounting periods so as to give a constant periodic rate of return on the 'net cash investment in the lease'. Net cash investment in the lease is a memorandum calculation and differs from net investment (the balance sheet figure) because the amount of cash invested in a lease will take account of cash flows other than rentals, such as taxation and funding costs. In the case of hire purchase, net cash investment in the lease will usually approximate to net investment.

Operating leases: all leases other than finance leases. The lessor will account for the asset as a fixed asset and include rentals received as income. The lessee will simply show rentals paid as an expense.

SSAP 22 GOODWILL

See section on group accounts.

SSAP 23 ACQUISITIONS AND MERGERS

See section on group accounts.

SSAP 24 PENSION CONTRIBUTIONS

Pension schemes are identified either as 'defined contribution' schemes, or 'defined benefit' schemes.

Defined contribution schemes:
do not provide any guaranteed amount of pension for the employee; pension will depend upon contributions and earnings of the fund. The employers cost is simply the contributions paid.

Defined benefit schemes:
provide a predetermined pension, usually based on the employees salary during the final year of employment. This makes it impossible for the employer to ensure in advance whether the regular contributions will be sufficient to fund the benefits promised. Periodic actuarial valuations are required which, among other things, should take account of any possible future increase of employees' earnings. These may result in employer having to provide further funds, or may indicate that past contributions have been excessive.

The effect of these 'experience deficiencies or surpluses' should not be treated as prior year adjustments. Variations from the regular pension costs, arising from actuarial valuations, should be allocated over the expected remaining service lives of employees in the scheme. This may involve making provisions if contributions are reduced as a result of a surplus, or prepayments if contributions are increased to cover a deficit. Some exceptions apply.

Group accounts

Strictly speaking, SSAPs 1 and 22 do not relate specifically to groups, but their provisions are most likely to be applicable in the case of groups. The institutional regulatory framework for groups is spread over SSAPs 1, 14, 22, and 23.

Initially, there were no prescribed formats for group accounts in the 1985 Companies Act because the EC Seventh Directive on group accounts (despite being adopted in 1983) had not been incorporated into UK law. The Companies Act 1989 deals with the form and content of group accounts by introducing Schedule 4A to the 1985 Act. Generally speaking, the effect of Schedule 4A is that the form and content of group accounts should correspond to those for a single company.

Other important changes introduced by the 1989 Act include revised definitions for parent and subsidiary companies, and exemption from the preparation of group accounts in the case of small and medium-sized groups.

SSAP 1 ASSOCIATED COMPANIES

An investment may fall to be treated as an associated company in two situations:

1) where the interest of the investor is that of a partner in a joint venture or consortium;
2) where the investment is long term and is substantial.

In both cases the investor must be able to exercise 'significant influence' over the financial and operational policy of the investee (e.g. by representation on the board). In the case of a long-term investment, this ability is presumed (subject to rebuttal) if the investment is 20% or more of the equity.

A form of partial consolidation is required called **equity accounting**. In consolidated accounts, dividends received by the investor are replaced by a share of the investee's profit for the period. The amount of such profits not received as a dividend (i.e. retained in the associate) is added to the carrying value of the investment. These adjustments are memorandum, the individual accounts of the investor are not affected.

The investment in the consolidated balance sheet must be shown as the total of:

Premium (or discount) on acquisition
(to the extent not written off)
plus
Share of net assets at the balance sheet date

Where none of the premium (or discount) has been written off, the total of these two items is the same as: cost of the investment plus share of post-acquisition profits retained in the associate – but see SSAP 22 on Goodwill.

If the investor is not part of a group (and consolidated accounts are not therefore prepared), the requirements of the standard should be achieved by presenting similar information on a memorandum basis.

SSAP 14 GROUP ACCOUNTS

Must be in the form of consolidated financial statements. Group accounts are not required if the holding company is a wholly owned subsidiary of another company.

Subsidiaries may be excluded from consolidation on the grounds of: (a) dissimilar activities; (b) lack of effective control; (c) severe restrictions of control; (d) if control is intended to be temporary.

Accounting for the investment in a subsidiary which has not been consolidated depends on the reason for its exclusion, namely: (a) dissimilar activities, include separate accounts of subsidiary; (b) lack of effective control, equity method; (c) severe restrictions of control, equity method at date when restrictions came into force; (d) temporary control, as a current asset at lower of cost and net realizable value.

Acquisitions and disposals of subsidiaries during the year:

Premium or discount on acquisition:
is the difference between purchase consideration and the underlying net assets (excluding goodwill) at fair value to the acquiring company. If fair values are not incorporated into the subsidiaries books, memorandum adjustments should be made for consolidation.

Results of subsidiary acquired:
provide sufficient information to enable shareholders to appreciate the effect on consolidated results.

Disposals:
include results up to date of date of disposal, and any gain (or loss) on sale of the investment. Profit (or loss) on sale to be calculated as the difference between:

sale proceeds, and
share of net assets at date of disposal together with premium or discount (to the extent it has not been written off) on acquisition.

Note that where the premium (or discount) on acquisition has not been written off, the second figure above will be the same as the cost of the investment plus the holding company's share of post-acquisition profits retained in the subsidiary (see similar concept regarding presentation of investments in associated companies as per SSAP 1 above).

SSAP 22 GOODWILL

Goodwill is the difference between the value of the business as a whole and the aggregate of the fair values of its separable net assets. Goodwill differs from other assets in that it is incapable of being realized as a separable asset and must be disposed of as part of the business.

Non-purchased goodwill should not be included in financial statements.

Purchased goodwill must not be carried as a permanent item and should be accounted for in one of two ways: (1) eliminated by immediate write off against reserves (preferred), or (2) amortized against profit on ordinary activities over the estimated useful economic life of the asset. Different acquisitions may be considered separately and either policy adopted. Goodwill arising on consolidation and Premiums on acquisition of associated companies are examples of purchased goodwill.

If the immediate write off is against unrealized reserves, an amount should be transferred to realized reserves on a systematic basis so as to maintain parity with the amortization basis.

Business combinations provide many opportunities for creative accounting. In view of this, the ASC has recently made it mandatory to disclose certain information in the accounts of the acquirer following an acquisition. These requirements have been incorporated into a revised version of SSAP 22.

SSAP 23 ACQUISITION AND MERGERS

The SSAP deals mainly with merger accounting. Roughly speaking, merger accounting is permitted where the combination results from an exchange of shares for shares. The four conditions which must be met before merger accounting is permitted are:

1) offer must be to all equity holders of the offeree company;
2) offeror must secure at least 90% of the equity of the offeree;
3) at least 90% of the consideration given must be in the form of equity in the offeror company;
4) immediately before the offer, the offeror did not hold 20% or more of the equity of the offeree company.

Any business combination which does not satisfy these requirements must be dealt with as an acquisition. The fair value of the consideration given must then be allocated according to the provisions in SSAP 14 and SSAP 22. The subsidiaries results must only be brought in from the date of acquisition.

Merger accounting is not possible unless the investment in the subsidiary is carried in the holding company's books at the nominal value of the shares issued. The effect of the Shearer v Bercain case is that the issue of such shares must be recorded at their fair value, the difference between fair value and nominal value being credited to share premium account. Sections 131 – 134 of the Companies Act provide a relief from this requirement (called merger relief) on a share for share exchange.

The merger relief provisions deal with accounting in the holding company's books and do not directly legislate for merger accounting, they simply make it possible. Merger relief is a relief from the requirement to record the share issue at fair value. The conditions attached to the relief are similar to, but less stringent than, those in SSAP 23 which permit merger accounting. There is no requirement for 90% of the total consideration to be in equity shares, and no corresponding provision regarding the 20% former holding.

Under merger accounting, the subsidiary's net assets are consolidated using book values, and consolidated profit (or loss) is not adjusted to exclude pre-acquisition profits. The effect is to combine the results as if the two companies had always been together.

Consolidation adjustments are required where the carrying value of the investment (being at nominal value of shares issued) differs from the total nominal value of shares acquired. Where the carrying value of the investment is less than the nominal value of the shares acquired, the difference is treated as a 'reserve on consolidation'. Where the carrying value of the investment exceeds the nominal value of the shares acquired, the difference is treated as a reduction of reserves; the word 'goodwill' must not be used because the fair value of the subsidiary's separable net assets have not been taken into account.

SSAP 20 FOREIGN SUBSIDIARIES

Notes for individual transactions are included in the general section. The provisions referred to will also apply to transactions with an overseas branch or subsidiary. The basis for translation of transactions is known as the 'temporal basis' and in certain cases is used for the translation of overseas financial statements.

Where the financial statements of an overseas entity require consolidation they must first be translated into sterling. The method of translation (and treatment of exchange differences) will depend upon the impact of currency movements on the cash flow of the investing company. This can be related to the operational relationship between the overseas entity (branch or subsidiary) and the investing company in UK.

If the trade of the overseas entity is independent of the investing company there is an investment in the net worth of that overseas entity which will remain until it is liquidated. Translation differences have no immediate impact on cash flows of the investing company. The closing rate method should be used and exchange gains or losses arising on translation must be recorded as movements on reserves.

Where the trade of the overseas entity is more dependent on the economic environment of the investing company's currency than its own, the overseas trade can be seen as an extension of transactions entered into by the investing company, e.g. where the overseas entity is acting as a selling agency for goods supplied by the investing company. Currency movements will have a recurring impact on the cash flows of the investing company. Translation should be on a temporal basis, and exchange gains or losses on translation treated as part of ordinary profit for the year.

When preparing accounts for consolidation, it will be necessary to deal with the translation of any outstanding foreign transactions first. This stage is usually referred to as the 'individual company stage' (in contrast to the translation required for consolidation purposes).

SSAP 10 IN RELATION TO GROUPS:

Based on group accounts. Unfortunately group accounts (being memorandum statements) include profits and adjustments which do not result in a corresponding change to group working capital, e.g.

1) the share of profits of associated companies which have been retained in the associate;
2) as regards the minority interests share of profit for the year, group working capital is affected to the extent that these profits have been retained (i.e. not paid to them as a dividend).

There are two ways in which the effect of these can be presented in the statement and they are discussed in more detail in the notes and illustrations for SSAP 10.

The effect of acquiring a subsidiary during the year can be shown either as a single application, or by including each individual class of asset and liability 'acquired' as part of the movements in the respective assets and liabilities of the group. In either case, a footnote should be given to provide a summary of the acquisition.

Students' SSAP Checklist

SSAP 1 Accounting for associated companies

Issued January 1971, amended August 1974, revised April 1982

Background

Business
The extension of operations through trade investments and in joint ventures or consortium arrangements had increased in popularity. Sometimes practical control existed if the other shares of the investee were widely dispersed amongst a disinterested public.

Accounting
By tradition only the cost of investments and dividend income was disclosed. Some companies started to increase disclosure on voluntary basis if investment was in a closely associated business.

Users
Growing interest in earnings (price-earnings ratio) as market indicator and for evaluation of business performance.

Law
Presentation of group accounts only necessary when a holding company and subsidiary relationship exists. CA 1967 increased the disclosure requirements of investments which exceeded 10% of the investee's equity.

Developing the standard

Points considered
Traditional accounting inadequate when investment creates a close interdependence of earnings.

Basic approach and method
Extend group accounts so as to include associates. Substitute dividends with share of earnings and impute difference to carrying value of investment. A form of partial consolidation called **equity accounting**.

Definitions

Associated company
Not a subsidiary. Partner in joint venture or consortium where investor is able to exercise significant influence; or the investment is substantial and long term with investor able to exercise significant influence.

Significant influence
Involves participation in financial and operational policy. Presumed if investment is 20% or more of equity voting capital unless shown otherwise, e.g. investee is also a subsidiary of a company external to reporting group. Test of 20% based on the aggregate of shares held by investing company together with the whole of those held by any of its direct or indirect subsidiaries. Holdings by associated companies are ignored.

The standard

INCOME AND INVESTMENT

Investing company's financial statements
Dividends received and receivable. Carrying value of investment not affected.

Investing group's consolidated financial statements
Substitute dividends with share of earnings. Difference imputed to carrying value of the investment which will then reflect the investing group's share in the 'equity' of investee.

Investing company which is not part of a group
Consolidated accounts are not required. Share of profits and equity value of investment to be presented in a supplementary memorandum statement on a basis similar to a group.

Presentation and disclosure

Profit and loss account
Investing group's share of:

Profits before tax as a single item.
Taxation as a single item separately within group charge.
Extraordinary items, aggregated with group's similar items or disclosed separately if material.
Other items (turnover etc) are normally not disclosed.

BALANCE SHEET

Investment

Investing company' own financial statements At cost less any amounts written off (unless at valuation).

Investing group's consolidated financial statements As total of:

1) a single amount for share of net assets (excluding goodwill) at balance sheet date after attributing, where possible, fair values to those at time of acquisition;
2) share of goodwill shown in associate's own accounts;
3) premium (goodwill) or discount on acquisition.

Items 2 and 3 may be amalgamated but item 1 separate.

Cross-references

CA 1985
Schedule 4A, introduced by the 1989 Companies Act, defines an associated undertaking in much the same way as SSAP 1, i.e. one in which there is a participating interest and the exercise of significant influence over the operational and financial policy. Significant influence is presumed where the holding is 20% or more of the voting rights. Associated companies must be accounted for under the equity method.

Standards
(i) SSAP 22, premium (discount) on acquisition, is example of purchased (or negative) goodwill. (ii) SSAP 14, equity accounting, required for certain subsidiaries excluded from consolidation. (iii) SSAP 3, earnings per share, includes earnings of associate. (iv) IAS 3 on consolidated financial statements deals with associated companies. The provisions are similar to SSAP 1 but definition does not mention joint venture or consortium.

Interesting points

Semantics
Equity is used to imply a **right to** a share of associate's earnings. If this is not received as a dividend there is an increase in the **equity stake** since retained earnings increase the associate's net assets. Changes in equity interest also occur when associate incurs losses.

Principles
Treatment in investing company's own accounts, including non-group investor, recognises separate entity concept and excludes unrealised profits. It also seems to recognise consolidation as a memorandum exercise.

Problems
(i) Group profits include amounts which cannot be distributed until they are received by the holding company. The same can be said to the extent that they include the subsidiary's profits but the holding company does control the dividend policy of a subsidiary. (ii) Group

asset values become a mixture of fair value and purchase cost, a problem of acquisition accounting generally.

Illustrations

MECHANICS OF EQUITY ACCOUNTING ONLY – NOT FULL PRESENTATION

Details

Investment
100 out of 400 ordinary shares; cost £200 on 1 Jan 1901

Reserves of associate:	
1 Jan 01	200
Profits after tax for year 01	140
Dividends paid during year	(40)
31 Dec 01	300

Net assets of associate:
There was no other capital or reserves and therefore net assets at each date were:

1 Jan 01	(400 + 200)	600
31 Dec 01	(400 + 300)	700

Assume book values are at fair value and do not include goodwill

INVESTING COMPANY'S OWN ACCOUNTS

Profits include £10 (25% of 40) dividend which is reflected by a cash flow and and increase of its own net assets

Investment remains at original cost   200

IN THE CONSOLIDATED ACCOUNTS

Share of profits reported (25% of 140)   35

Represented by:
Own asset increase through cash flows (dividend)   10
and
Share of associate's increase in net assets
25% of £100 (retained profits for year)   25

The £25 is dealt with by increasing the carrying value of the investment making it (200 + 25) £225. This is reflected by increasing the net asset element in the presentation:

Investment
The premium on acquisition is £50 as follows:

Cost of investment:	200
Less interest in net assets (25% of 600)	150
	50

Presentation outline:

1 Jan 01		31 Dec 01
50	Premium on acquisition	50
150	Share of net assets	175
200	Total	225

Notes

SSAP 2 Disclosure of accounting policies

Issued November 1971

Background

Business
Tended to be insular from accounting developments. Absence of any codified accounting practice may have encouraged abuse, or arbitrary use, of accounting principles.

Accounting
Problems of flexibility over application of principles were debated in professional press. The credibility of the profession was eroded following publicized cases in late 1960s. The ASSC was formed.

Law
Disclosure of policies not required except that CA 1948 did provide for disclosure of the effect of any changes 'in basis of accounting'. Tax laws may have had an influence on the choice of policies used.

Developing the standard

Points considered
Diversity of business precludes a rigid approach to SSAPs. Many companies were not justifying, reviewing or disclosing their policies.

Basic approach and method
Minimize flexibility through SSAPs. Disclosure of accounting policies should improve the information in accounts and also force directors to select and adopt specific policies. Policies adopted should be disclosed by way of notes to the accounts.

Definitions

Fundamental accounting concepts
Broad basic assumptions. Four with general acceptability, i.e. going concern, accruals, consistency, prudence.

Going concern
Business will continue operational existence into foreseeable future. No intention to liquidate or curtail activities.

Accruals
Revenue and costs recognised when earned or incurred and not when exchanged in cash, subject to exercise of prudence. Match revenues with costs within the same period where their relationship is reasonably established.

Consistency
Of treatment for like items within each period and from one to the next.

Prudence
Gains not recognized until either they are realized or realization is reasonably certain. Provide all known losses even when amount is uncertain.

Accounting bases
Methods developed for applying fundamental concepts.

Accounting policies
Specific bases chosen and adopted by management.

The standard

Fundamental concepts
Observation presumed unless a clear statement otherwise. Disclose departures, e.g. a change of policy is a departure from consistency.

Accounting policies
If judged material or critical disclose by way of note to the accounts. Clear, fair and brief explanations.

Presentation and disclosure

Practice
The SSAP simply states 'by way of note to the accounts'. In earlier practices this was usually Note 1 but more recently separate page(s) without a note number have been used and the relevant page number(s) are referred to in directors' adoption and auditor's report.

Cross references

CA 1985
Disclosure of accounting policies is required as 'notes to the accounts'. Observation of the four fundamental accounting concepts required but

they are called 'accounting principles' and a fifth has been added which is called 'separate valuation of assets and liabilities'.

Standards
(i) Revised SSAP 6 and revised SSAP 12 for identifying situations which constitute a change of accounting policy. (ii) The introduction of a new SSAP could precipitate a change of policy. (iii) SSAPs which deal with particular accounting bases require disclosure of the policy adopted. (iv) IAS 1 treats prudence as a practical consideration and not a concept; see below.

Interesting points

Semantics
(i) Problem with usage of terms: principles, practices, conventions, rules, methods, procedures, and concepts are recognized in the SSAP. Bases, policies, and four concepts are singled out and defined. (ii) It can be argued that 'prudence' is not a concept but a common-sense working rule along with 'materiality' and 'substance over form' as set out in IAS 1. (iii) Development of SSAPs may reveal other concepts such as 'all inclusive' in SSAP 6.

Principles
(i) The purpose of the SSAP was not to develop any basic accounting theory, footnote to para 1. (ii) The main difficulty in applying the fundamental concepts relates to transactions which are spread over a number years such as stocks, fixed assets, research and development. (iii) Choice of bases diminish as standards become established.

Problems
(i) The priority of prudence over accruals is sometimes contradicted by SSAPs, e.g. see SSAP 9 on production overheads. (ii) SSAP 2 could eventually become obsolete through the progressive publication of standards. Most areas mentioned in SSAP 2 as being subject to different accounting bases are covered by a subsequent SSAP which requires disclosure of the policy adopted.

Illustration

Example and analysis of an accounting policy note.

DEVELOPMENT EXPENDITURE

Development expenditure attributable to projects whose technical feasibility and commercial viability are reasonably assured is capitalized and amortized over a maximum of the first three years' sales. Research expenditure is written off in the year during which it is incurred.

SSAP 2 ANALYSIS OF THE NOTE

Concepts

Accruals – matching development costs with related sales
and
Prudence – writing off research costs as incurred in view of uncertainty
of relationship to future income.

Bases

Possible choice between:

1)   write off all expenditure as incurred; or

2)   write off all research costs but capitalize (and amortize) certain
     development costs if criteria in SSAP 13 satisfied.

Policy

Adoption of the second of the two bases.

Analysis of the policy

The above policy note is based on one found in the published financial
statements of Hestair plc. SSAP 13 requires the amortization period or
rate to be considered on an individual project basis. Hestair seems
to have chosen a three-year basis for all projects, perhaps this bears
some relationship to conditions which exist in the industry concerned.

   If, during the three-year period, sale of one of the projects is
abandoned the unamortised expenditure must be written off immediately. The company would then have to consider whether the
write-off is as an 'exceptional item' under SSAP 6.

Notes

SSAP 3   Earnings per share

Issued February 1971, revised August 1974.

Background

Users
Earnings had become the single most important indicator of a company's performance. The price-earnings (PE) ratio had become the most commonly used stock market indicator and was being used on a world-wide basis. The earnings per share (EPS) on which the PE ratio was based needed to be calculated and disclosed on a comparable basis but no standard practice existed.

Developing the standard

Points considered
Lack of comparability because of different definitions of earnings. Trends in EPS as between one period and the next are important and therefore a prescription needed to deal with comparatives when there have been changes in share capital. The UK tax system sometimes causes post-tax profit to vary according to the level of distribution, e.g. when ACT is irrecoverable.

Basic approach and method
Earnings to be based on those available for equity shareholders before extraordinary items. Revise comparatives when bonus shares issued and for the bonus element in rights issue. EPS to be based primarily on earnings after all tax charges and no adjustment is needed for items of tax which vary with level of distribution unless they are significant. Disclose EPS on face of profit and loss account.

Definitions

Earnings
Consolidated profit after: tax, minority interests, and preference dividend but before extraordinary items.

Earnings per share
Divide earnings by the number equity shares in issue and ranking for dividend in the period.

Diluted earnings per share
Denominator includes maximum equity shares ranking in future (e.g. includes any which will rank on conversion of convertible loan stock in issue). Earnings may require adjustment to reflect variations which would occur if dilution took place, e.g. elimination of loan interest.

Tax element
Can be classified into 'constant' and 'variable' as follows:

Constant   Those not affected by level of distribution such as corporation tax and tax credits on franked investment income.

Variable   Those which can vary according to level of distributions such as irrecoverable ACT, and unrelieved overseas tax where distributions restrict the tax credit.

EPS on net basis
All tax charges, both constant and variable, included.

EPS on nil basis
Exclude variable element of tax charge.

The standard

Earnings per share
All listed companies to disclose on a net basis. The EPS on a nil basis also disclosed if materially different from net basis. Disclose diluted EPS if dilution is 5% or more of the basic EPS.

Presentation and disclosure

Earnings per share
On face of profit and loss account even when negative (loss per share). Basis either in the profit and loss account or in the notes. Corresponding amounts for previous year.

Fully diluted EPS
To have equal prominence if disclosed. Where calculations result in a figure higher than basic (e.g. due to adjustments for interest) the amount should not be shown. Diluted EPS not required if basic is negative and as dilution relates to future events it would not normally be meaningful to apply it to comparatives.

Changes in equity assuming new shares rank for dividend

The following summary is based on guidance notes in Appendix 1 of the SSAP.

Bonus issue
Treat as if in issue throughout whole period. Also revise previous year's as if in issue throughout the whole of that period.

Issue at full market price
Infrequent. New capital provides increased earning capacity from date of receipt therefore denominator for current year should be weighted average shares in issue. No revision of comparatives.

Rights issue
Like an issue at full price with a bonus element. Revision of comparatives required for bonus element. Current year's denominator determined as if bonus element in issue throughout whole period and full price element on a weighted average.

Suggested formula for rights issues
In the appendix to SSAP 3 this is based on two factors, namely:

1) *Theoretical ex rights price (TERP)*. See illustration for explanation;
2) *Actual cum rights price (ACRP)* for the last day of trading cum rights.

These are then used as follows:

Comparatives   The original EPS multiplied by the factor TERP ÷ ACRP so as to adjust for the bonus element.
Current year's denominator   The weighted average number of shares in issue up to date of issue is multiplied by the factor ACRP ÷ TERP (the reciprocal) and the result added to the weighted average number of shares in issue after the rights issue.

Share exchange on takeover
Assume the shares were issued at beginning of the period which first includes the new subsidiary's earnings.

DILUTED EARNINGS PER SHARE

May have to be calculated where:

1) Separate classes of equity do not rank for dividend in period but will do so in future;
2) Debentures, loan stock, or preference shares, are convertible into equity shares in the future;
3) Options or warrants to subscribe for equity shares are outstanding.

In the case of a separate class of equity, the diluted EPS is calculated on the basis that the shares ranked for dividend from the beginning of the period. Shares of the same class as existing equity, which are treated separately for some reason (e.g. issued towards the end of the period and not entitled to dividends for that period) should not be treated as a separate class.

In the case of convertible debentures etc., earnings should be adjusted by adding back the assumed interest savings (net of corporation tax).

In the case of options or warrants, assume the maximum number are exercised on the first day of the period (or date of issue if later) and that earnings are increased by a notional sum equal to what have been earned had the subscription proceeds been received and invested in 2½% Consolidated Stock at the closing price for the previous day.

Diluted EPS need only be disclosed if dilution is material. Dilution amounting to 5% or more is regarded as material.

Cross references

Standards
Most SSAPs affect the calculation of earnings, see in particular SSAP 1 regarding associated companies and SSAP 6 which defines extraordinary items. SSAPs 8 and 15 deal with the tax element. There is no equivalent IAS.

Interesting points

Principles
An interesting comment is made in Appendix 1 which states that transfers to a sinking fund, even if supported by cash transfers, only divide profits between those available now and those available later (i.e. they do not reduce earnings for the period). Students should be able to relate this to certain points in their book-keeping studies on sinking funds.

Illustrations

1) The following show how trends would be distorted if comparatives were not revised following changes in share capital.

Basic EPS

1901		1902	Trend
£16	Earnings for equity shares	£20	
100	Number of equity shares	100	
16p	EPS	20p	25% up

Bonus issue of 1 for 1 on 1st Jul 1902 – profits remain same:

100	Shares 1 Jan.	100
—	Bonus issue 1 Jul 1902	100
100	Shares 31 Dec	200

| 16p | EPS if 1901 not revised | 10p | 37.5% down? |
| 8p | EPS with 1901 revised | 10p | 25% up |

Additional capital of £50 1 Jul 1902 – profits 1902 up by £5.
Market value of shares at time of new issue = £1 per share

(a) If the £50 is raised by an issue of 50 shares at full market price:

£16	Earnings for equity shares	£25	
	Denominators:		
	100 × 6/12ths	50	
	150 × 6/12ths	75	
100		125	
16p	EPS (1901 not affected)	20p	25% up

(b) If the £50 is raised by rights issue 1 for 1 at price of 50P each:

Calculate theoretical ex rights price:

100 at £1	£100
100 at 50p	50
200 (75p each)	150

Denominators:

	100 × 6/12ths × 100/75	66.66
	200 × 6/12ths	100.00
100		166.66

| 16p | EPS if 1901 not revised | 15p | 6.25% down? |
| 12p | 1901 revised (16p × 75/100) | 15p | 25% up |

Aide memoire: Revision of previous year always results in a lower EPS due to bonus element. As TERP will be less than ACRP the factor must be TERP ÷ ACRP. The reciprocal (ACRP ÷ TERP) is used in current year.

2) Diluted EPS when convertible debentures are outstanding

Ordinary shares in issue and entitled to dividend at accounting date: 1,000,000
Profits after tax, minority interests, and preference dividend: £200,000
Convertible 10% debentures in issue at accounting date: £500,000.
These are convertible into ordinary shares as follows:

in two year's time at 125 ordinary shares for each £100 nominal stock;

in three year's time at 110 ordinary shares for each £100 nominal stock.

Corporation tax rate is 35%.

Basic EPS (£200,000 ÷ 1,000,000) 20p

Diluted EPS:
    Adjusted earnings:
    Current earnings   £200,000
    Add: Interest savings (10% × £500,000 × 0.65)   32,500

                                         232,500

Maximum number of shares:
    Current   1,000,000
    Conversions (5,000 × 125)   625,000

                                       1,625,000

Diluted EPS (£232,500 ÷ 1,625,000) 14.31p
Dilution is greater than 5% of basic and should be disclosed.

3) Diluted EPS when share options outstanding

Ordinary shares in issue and entitled to dividend at 31 December 01:
1,000,000.
Earnings in year ended 31 December 01 available for these shares:
£200,000.
Share options had been granted on 1 July 01 to subscribe for 100,000
ordinary shares at a price of 50p each. No options had been exercised
by 31 December. The price of Consolidated Stock on 30 June 01 was £20
per £100.
Corporation tax rate is 35%.

Basic EPS (£200,000 ÷ 1,000,000) 20p
Diluted EPS
    Adjusted earnings:
    Current earnings   £200,000
    Add: Notional income for 6 months on 2½% Consols
        6/12 × 2½% × (£50,000 ÷ 0.2) × 0.65   2,031

                                         202,031

Weighted average number of shares:
    6/12 × 1,000,000   500,000
    6/12 × 1,100,000   550,000

                                       1,050,000

Diluted EPS (202,031 ÷ 1,050,000) = 19.24p. Since dilution is not
material (it is less than 5%) disclosure is not required.

Notes

SSAP 4 The accounting treatment of government grants

Issued April 1974, now under revision through ED43

Background

Companies in development areas were receiving regional development grants but different views were held by accountants on treatment of capital based grants.

Government assistance in the form of grants has greatly increased, in variety and form, since the SSAP was issued. The ASC has therefore proposed substantial revision through ED 43, issued June 1988. Some of the proposed amendments are mentioned under 'Interesting points' at the end of these notes.

Developing the standard

Points considered

Revenue based grants do not cause accounting problems, they are simply matched with the related costs. There are three different views regarding capital based grants, namely:

1) credit to profit immediately;
2) credit to non-distributable reserve as permanent item;
3) credit to profit over the useful life of the related asset either as a deferred credit or through a reduction of depreciation.

Basic approach and method

The first two methods do not articulate with the treatment of related expenditure. The third correlates treatment of grant with amortization of expenditure and is the most appropriate. Can be applied in one of two ways and both are permitted.

The standard

Capital grants

To be credited to profit over expected useful life of asset either by:

1) reducing cost of asset and depreciating the reduced amount. This has the advantage of simplicity;

2) carrying grant on a deferred credit account and releasing to profit annually at the same rate as related depreciation. This method has the advantage of recording all fixed assets on a uniform basis.

Presentation and disclosure

Deferred credit basis
If chosen the balance should be shown separately in the balance sheet but not as part of shareholders' funds.

Cross-references

CA 1985
(i) Balance sheet formats include an item called 'accruals and deferred income' which is suitable for the balance of deferred credit. (ii) Crediting the asset may violate requirement to show fixed assets at purchase price; see below.

Standards
(i) SSAP 21 deals with effect of grants on recognition of income from leased assets. (ii) IAS 20 on government grants accords closely to SSAP 4 but includes a provision for grant repayments to be treated as a correction to an accounting estimate, in which case SSAP 6 would be relevant.

Interesting points

Principles
(i) Effect on profit of either method identical. As there appears to be no theoretical basis for a choice the ASC could have made an arbitrary rule for the sake of consistency. (ii) Crediting the grant to cost of asset may now be a departure from the CA 1985 requirement to show fixed assets at 'purchase price'. This requirement did not exist at the time the SSAP was introduced.

ED 43 PROPOSED AMENDMENTS

The alternative which allows capital based grants to be deducted from the cost of related assets is to be removed. The ASC accept that the deduction from asset approach could be in conflict with CA 1985 (see above). In view of the many types of grant available, an appendix has been suggested giving appropriate treatment of certain grants. In general terms, grants would be matched with the expenditure towards which they contribute. Some grants are given on condition that they are treated as share capital, such grants should be credited direct to undistributable reserves. This provision adds to the number of items which may be taken direct to reserves without passing through the profit and loss account (see SSAP 6).

Illustration

The following illustrates how both methods have the same effect on reported profits.

Cost of asset with 10 year life £1,000. Depreciated straight line. Grant received £100.

COMPARISON OF METHODS

	Reduce asset cost	*Deferred credit*
1) Balance sheet items:		
Asset at purchase cost	£1,000	£1,000
Grant received	(100)	—
Carrying value	900	1,000
Depreciation	(90)	(100)
Net book value carried forward	810	900
Deferred credit (grant received)	—	(100)
Credited to profit	—	10
Deferred credit carried forward	—	(90)
Net balances	810	810
2) Profit and loss account items:		
Depreciation charge	£90	£100
Deferred credit	—	(10)
Total	90	90

Note that ED 43 proposes to remove this choice of method, and the deferred credit basis must be used.

Notes

SSAP 5 Accounting for value added tax

Issued April 1974, revised June 1975

Background

Business
On the introduction of VAT the business community became a collector of tax for the Customs and Excise. A business registered for VAT must charge VAT on its taxable outputs. It will also be charged VAT on most of its inputs. The business is then required to account to Customs and Excise on a quarterly basis for the tax on outputs less the tax on inputs. In some cases the VAT on inputs is non-deductible (e.g. on cars and UK entertaining).

Accounting
Disclosure requirements at time required 'turnover' to be shown by way of note to the accounts, not as part of the profit calculation as under the CA 1985 formats.

The standard is on presentation and disclosure

Turnover
Exclude VAT. May be disclosed gross with relevant VAT deducted.

Non-deductible inputs
Include VAT as part of the cost of the relevant inputs. Where trade is partially exempt and input VAT is apportioned the residue falling as a cost on the trader should be included with related items, estimates where appropriate.

Balances
Amounts due to, or recoverable from, Customs and Excise are not required to be disclosed separately.

Cross references

CA 1985
Balance sheet formats include an item called 'other creditors including

taxation and social security'. The amount due to Customs and Excise for VAT falls under this heading.

Standards
There is no equivalent IAS.

Interesting points

Has SSAP 5 become redundant? The book-keeping automatically deals with the problem now that turnover is not simply a memorandum note in the published accounts. The CA 1985 formats deal with disclosure of balances.

Illustration

The effect of non-recoverable input tax on partially exempt trader:

		Sales	VAT
Outputs:	Subject to VAT (including zero rated)	30,000	3,600
	Exempt supplies	10,000	—
	Total	40,000	3,600

		Costs	
Inputs:	Traceable to non-exempt outputs	20,000	2,400
	Non-traceable (e.g. telephone, stationery)	4,000	600
	Total	24,000	3,000

The whole of the £2,400 input VAT can be set against the £3,600 output VAT. Turnover shows only 3/4 of the outputs are subject to VAT and therefore only 3/4 of the remaining £600 (£450) can be set against output VAT. The balance of £150 must be allocated amongst the various costs to which it relates.

Notes

SSAP 6   Extraordinary items and prior year adjustments

*Issued April 1971, revised
June 1974, revised August
1986*

Background

Business
Considered profit should only reflect the ordinary day-to-day items. Tended to hide non-recurrent losses in reserves (reserve accounting) but to inflate profits with non-recurrent profits. Reorganization costs in recent years gave problems over interpretation of the original SSAP 6.

Accounting
No uniform practice until first SSAP 6, then inconsistency between companies in their classification of extraordinary and exceptional items. Some later SSAPs required practices inconsistent with the original SSAP 6.

Law
CA 1967 (at time of original SSAP 6) required disclosure of the effect on profit from exceptional non-recurrent items, from items not usually undertaken, and from changes in accounting policy. CA 1981 codified parts of first SSAP 6.

Developing the standard

Points considered
Two views commonly expressed called: (i) 'current operating performance concept' which excludes non-recurring items from reported profits and (ii) 'all inclusive concept' where all profits and losses are included but may require separate disclosure. Excluding non-recurring items is not desirable because:

1) loss of comparability between companies since exclusion of items from profit becomes a matter of subjective judgement;
2) excluded items may be overlooked when reviewing series of years;
3) the all-inclusive concept of profit gives better view of performance.

Basic approach and method

The 'all-inclusive concept' to be applied. All items, even if related to prior year, to be reflected in profits for the year except:

1) prior year adjustments as defined;
2) those permitted or required by law and SSAPs to be taken direct to reserves.

Profit statement to be divided between ordinary and extraordinary activities. All reserve movements to be in one place.

Definitions

Ordinary activities

Those usually, frequently, and regularly undertaken and any related activities incidental or arising therefrom. They include, but are not confined to, trading.

Exceptional items

Material items which derive from ordinary activities and need, by virtue of their size or incidence, to be disclosed separately if the accounts are to give a true and fair view.

Extraordinary items

Material items which derive from events outside ordinary activities. Do not include exceptional items, nor do they include prior year items merely because related to prior year.

Prior year adjustments

Material items which arise from changes of accounting policy or the correction of fundamental errors. They do not include adjustments which arise from the correction of prior year accounting estimates.

Business segment

An identifiable component whose results are distinguishable from the remainder. Normally separate product lines or markets.

Examples

Exceptional

Redundancy costs of a continuing segment; reorganization costs not related to discontinuance; abnormal charges such as bad debts and stock write-offs; insurance claims; adjustments on sale of fixed assets unless it arises out of an event which is extraordinary; writing off intangibles except as part of normal amortization; transfers to employee share schemes.

Extraordinary

Discontinuance of business segment through termination or sale; sale of investment not acquired with intention of resale; expropriation of assets; adjustments on sale of fixed assets if event extraordinary.

The standard

All items
Must be recognized in profit and loss for year unless permitted or required by law or accounting standards to be taken direct to reserves.

Tax
Attributable to extraordinary items must also treated as extraordinary and should be calculated as the difference between total tax on whole results and tax on the ordinary profit.

Presentation and disclosure

Profit and loss account
Show separately in the order of: profit on ordinary activities; extraordinary profits or losses; profit for the financial year; appropriations.

Exceptional
By way of note or where necessary for a true and fair view show on the face of profit and loss account (revised SSAP 6). See illustration.

Extraordinary
After profit on ordinary activities after tax. Each item shown individually or detailed by way of note. Where appropriate the attributable tax and minority interests share should be shown.

Prior year adjustments
Adjust opening balance of retained profits. Restate comparatives.

Reserves
Statement of all movements in one place. If not at foot of profit and loss account make a reference as to where it can be found (revised SSAP 6).

Cross-references

CA 1985
Now refers to extraordinary and exceptional items but does not define them. Formats prescribe manner of disclosure. There is no conflict with SSAP 6.

Standards
(i) SSAP 6 is important in relation to other standards, e.g. SSAP 3 where EPS is based on profits before extraordinary items and SSAP 14 where profit on sale of a subsidiary is likely to be extraordinary. (ii) IAS 8 accords closely to SSAP 6 but uses the term 'unusual items' instead of extraordinary. The term 'exceptional' is not used but the same principle is discussed by referring to items 'typical of the ordinary activities' which are 'abnormal' in size and frequency. Also see comments under 'interesting points' below dealing with the IAS 8 suggestion on a change of policy.

Interesting points

Semantics
Change of policy arises from choice between more than one base and does not include the modification (or refinement) of an existing policy. The arguments are based on definitions in SSAP 2. For example.the fundamental concept which must be applied to most fixed asset costs is accruals (matching) and the method developed (base) for this is depreciation. This implies that there is no choice of base and therefore a change in method of calculating depreciation is not a change of policy.

See SSAP 12 and earlier commentary in this book under the section called 'A Change of Policy'.

IAS 8 suggests that where it is difficult to establish whether an adjustment results from a change of policy or a revision of an estimate it should be treated as a revision of an estimate.

Principles
(i) Change of policy is only permitted where the new policy is justified on the grounds of fairer presentation, e.g. as might be the case on introduction of a new SSAP. (ii) Terminated activities are extraordinary even if spread or occur over a number of periods as a result of a single or series of decisions.

Notice how the standards generally have tried to persuade against treating an adjustment as a change of policy. This presumably flows from a consideration of prudence since if the adjustment is classed as a change of policy the effect on previous years can be left out of the profits for the current year.

Illustrations

The following outline format includes an exceptional item presented on the face of the profit and loss account. The revised SSAP 6 states this may be necessary in some cases to show a true and fair view. Alternatively it can be amalgamated with earlier items in the statement and disclosed in the notes.

	Note		
Turnover	1		500,000
Cost of sales	2		300,000
Gross profit			200,000
Other operating expenses	3		50,000
Trading profit before exceptional item			150,000
Exceptional item	4		40,000
			110,000
Investment income	5	14,000	
Interest payable	6	10,000	

		4,000
Profit on ordinary activities before tax		114,000
Taxation	7	44,000
Profit on ordinary activities after tax		70,000
Minority interests		3,000
Profit before extraordinary item		67,000
Extraordinary loss after taxation	8	10,000
Profit for financial year		57,000
Dividends	9	25,000
Retained profit for year		32,000

Movements on reserves are detailed in Note 10

Extracts from Notes:

4) Exceptional item – describe e.g. abnormal write-off of obsolete stocks.

8) Extraordinary item:

Loss on disposal of investment in subsidiary	14,000
Tax relief thereon (see below)	4,000
	10,000

10) Movement on reserves:

	Distributable	Undistributable
Balance at 1 January	220,000	96,000
Prior year adjustment (describe)	20,000	
As restated	200,000	
Surplus on revaluation of properties		64,000
Retained profit for year	32,000	
Balance at 31 December	232,000	160,000

Tutorial note: The taxation attributable to the extraordinary loss would have been found as follows:

Tax on all transactions for the year	40,000
Tax on ordinary activities	44,000
Therefore tax relief on extraordinary item	4,000

Notes

Notes

SSAP 8   The treatment of taxation under the imputation system

Issued August 1974,
appendix 3 added December 1977

Introductory comment

This standard was issued soon after introduction of the new tax and contains a number of matters which accountants would normally have solved themselves by a simple application of general principles. It is difficult to see how some items, such as payment of ACT, could have been accounted for differently to that required in the standard.

Payment of ACT is simply what it says: an advance payment of the corporation tax for the year. It is paid shortly after payment of a dividend and becomes primarily a payment on account of the corporation tax for the year in which the dividend was paid although there are provisions for setting it off against liabilities for other periods (previous and subsequent) if tax for the current year is not sufficient.

Payments on account to a creditor are never treated as an expense item under the accruals concept. The full liability incurred is expensed and payments on account are merely reductions of the amount owing. There is no reason to treat the taxation expense differently, although it is a different matter if the ACT is considered to be irrecoverable for some reason.

The following notes deal mainly with those matters which appear to justify why the standard was needed.

Developing the standard

Dividends received
Two possibilities, namely:

1) credit profit with cash received, i.e. ignoring tax credit;
2) credit profit with Franked Investment Income (FII), i.e. cash received plus tax credit and treat the tax credit as component of tax charge.

Second method preferred as it articulates with other elements of profit which are dealt with on a pre-tax and post-tax basis.

ACT on proposed dividends

The Companies Act (and matching) require proposed dividends to be shown as a liability, therefore the related ACT which will be payable as a result should also be shown as a liability (articulation).

Irrecoverable ACT

Two possibilities, namely:

1) treat as component part of the tax charge;
2) since it stems from the payment of dividends treat as an appropriation.

First method preferred. It constitutes a tax expense of the company not of the shareholders and therefore is not an appropriation.

Definitions

Recoverable ACT

That which can be set off against a liability for corporation tax, or properly against the deferred tax account.

Irrecoverable ACT

Any ACT other than recoverable.

Franked investment income

Cash dividends received from other UK companies plus the tax credit.

The standard including presentation

Taxation in profit and loss account

Where material the following should be disclosed separately:

1) corporation tax on income (including any transfers to or from deferred tax account);
2) tax attributable to FII;
3) irrecoverable ACT;
4) unrelieved overseas tax.

If the rate of corporation tax is not known use (and disclose) latest rate.

Outgoing dividends

Should not include related ACT in the profit and loss account.

Dividends received

From other UK companies show as as FII (i.e cash received plus tax credit) and include tax credit as a component of the tax charge.

Proposed dividends

Include in current liabilities without related ACT.

ACT on proposed dividends

Provide for and include under current liabilities. If the related ACT is recoverable (e.g. against next year's corporation tax) it should be deducted from deferred tax account or, where there is no deferred tax account, shown as a deferred asset.

Cross-references

CA 1985
Formats prescribe manner of disclosure for investment income, for tax on profits, and taxation liabilities. There is no conflict with SSAP 8. The ACT recoverable on proposed dividends could be included under the item 'Prepayments and accrued income' if there is no deferred tax account.

Standards
(i) SSAP 3 nil and net basis for EPS. (ii) SSAP 15 deferred tax. (iii) SSAP 6 for revision of prior year estimates. (iv) There is no equivalent international standard. IAS 12 'Accounting for taxes on income' is mainly concerned with deferred tax.

Interesting points

Semantics
There is no mention in SSAP 8 of under- or over-provisions of tax in previous year and this infers that it is simply included in tax on income since it arises from a revision of an estimate made in the previous year (see SSAP 6). Maybe separate disclosure would sometimes be required so as to show a true and fair view.

Principles
Adjustments for deferred tax are only disclosed in the profit and loss account if material, otherwise include them with total for tax on income. Movements on the deferred tax account account must in any case be disclosed under SSAP 15. Appendix 1 suggests that detailed disclosure of the tax charge, except for simple cases, should be by way of note.

Illustration

A company has a 31 March accounting date. Although it started trading in 1958, it has by now passed through the transition period allowed in the 1987 Finance Act and pays its mainstream corporation tax nine months after the end of each period. At 1 April 1989 the relevant balances brought forward were:

Corporation tax for year ending 31 March 1989		260,000
Dividends payable		14,000
ACT payable		6,000
Deferred tax:		
Unreversed timing differences	126,000	
Less recoverable ACT	6,000	120,000

During year ended 31 March 1990 the rate of ACT is 3/7ths. and the following occurred:

1) Paid the proposed dividend brought forward, paid an interim dividend of £28,000 and proposed a final dividend of £56,000.
2) Received a dividend from another UK company of £2,800 (cash amount).
3) Paid ACT on due dates. Total amount for year is calculated as follows:

Dividends paid (14,000 + 28,000)	42,000
Less dividends received	2,800
	39,200

ACT 3/7ths × 39,200 = £16,800

4) Agreed with the Inland Revenue that the mainstream corporation tax due for year ending 31 March 1989 was £263,000 and paid this on the 1 January 1990. Estimated corporation tax for current year at £290,000. Transferred £12,000 to deferred tax account.

The extracts from the financial statements would be as follows:

Profit and loss account:

Franked investment income (2,800 + 1,200)		4,000
Profit on ordinary activities before tax		?
Taxation:		
Corporation tax on income – estimated at 00%	293,000	
(290,000 + 3,000 underprovided previous year)		
Transfer to deferred tax account	12,000	
Tax credits on Franked Investment Income	1,200	306,200
Profit on ordinary activities after tax		?
Dividends: Interim paid	28,000	
Final proposed	56,000	84,000

Tutorial note: Details of the tax charge are usually given in a Note to Financial Statements.

Balance sheet:
Creditors falling due within one year:

Taxation (mainstream 1989/90 £290,000 − ACT paid of £16,800	
+ ACT payable on proposed dividend 24,000)	297,000
Proposed dividends	56,000

Provision for liabilities and charges:

Deferred tax account (£126,000 + 12,000 − ACT on	
proposed dividend 24,000)	114,000

Tutorial note: ACT is first treated as an advance payment of corporation tax for the year during which the dividend was paid – not the year to which the dividend relates.

Notes

SSAP 9 Stocks and work in progress – excluding long-term contracts

Issued May 1975, revised September 1988

The notes for specific matters relating to long-term contracts are dealt with separately. The following relates to stocks and work in progress generally. Most of the changes made to SSAP 9 in 1988 were related to long-term contracts.

Background

Business
Stocks are a significant element in profit measurement. Research indicates that the average ratio of stock to pre-tax profits is 4 to 1. Marginal costing preferred by many companies.

Accounting
Practices varied quite widely. The general principle of 'lower of cost and net realizable value' was accepted but no agreement over whether cost should be on a 'marginal' or 'absorbed' basis. Recommendation by ICAEW (No. 22) was not conducive to including fixed overheads.

Law
Legal requirements concerning stocks did change as between the CA 1948 (which governed accounting at the time of the original SSAP) and CA 1985. The 1985 Act requires (under the historical cost accounting rules) that current assets should be at purchase price or production cost, together with an additional provision to include them at net realizable value if lower. See further points under 'Cross-references'.

Developing the standard

Points considered
Many problems such as the choice of cost accounting method (e.g. job or process) and cost identification (FIFO etc), are of a practical nature

rather than matters of principle. Differences of principle relate more to the treatment of fixed overheads and abnormal items in manufactured cost.

Basic approach and method

Stocks normally need to be stated at the lower of cost or net realizable value (NRV). In cases where estimated replacement price is lower than NRV, it is not acceptable to reduce stocks to replacement price since this would take account of a loss greater than that which will be incurred. Replacement price may sometimes given an indication of NRV.

Matching requires that cost of stock should include production overheads including those that accrue on a time basis. Abnormal costs should be excluded so that cost of inefficiency is not carried forward in stock.

Definitions

Stocks

Comprise: goods purchased for resale; consumable stores; raw materials and components used in manufacture of goods for resale; products (and services) in intermediate stages of completion; long-term contracts; finished goods.

Cost

All expenditure in the NORMAL course of business in bringing stock to present location and condition. Includes purchase and conversion costs.

Cost of purchase

Includes purchase price, import duties, transport, handling, and any other directly attributable costs, less trade discounts.

Cost of conversion

Includes direct labour, sub-contracting costs, production overheads (defined), other attributable overheads which service production.

Production overheads

Includes those accruing on time basis. They should be absorbed on the basis of the NORMAL level of production.

Net realizable value

Estimated (or known) selling price less the costs of completion and costs of marketing, selling and distributing.

The standard

Basis

Aggregate of lower of cost and net realizable value of the separate items of stock and work in progress.

Disclosure

Accounting policy. Stocks sub-classified into the main groups as required by standard balance sheet formats (adapted where appropriate) in CA 1985.

Guidance on practical problems

Normal course of business

Abnormal costs such as excessive spoilage and idle capacity should be excluded as they are not costs incurred in the normal course of business in bringing stock to its existing state and location.

Overheads

It is the function of an overhead and not its variance with time which is the distinguishing characteristic. Production overhead allocation should be based on normal capacity (i.e. in normal course of business).

Normal capacity

Consider technical facilities, budgeted levels, achieved levels during current and previous years.

Central services

General management costs (as distinct from functional) to be excluded. Costs which service the production function (e.g. stock control) to be included.

Costing methods

There are two main problems, namely:

1) cost accounting method such as job and process costing;
2) cost selection methods (FIFO etc) when costs are constantly changing.

Judgement must be exercised by management to select methods which give the fairest practicable approximation to cost. Consider:

Base stock and LIFO   Costs derived from these methods are not usually appropriate for stock valuation because they result in amounts that bear little relationship to recent cost levels.

Standard costs   Permitted if regularly reviewed and revised.

Other methods   Latest price to all units in stock is not acceptable since it could result in recognizing an unrealized profit. Selling price less profit margin may be satisfactory in the absence of a cost accounting system.

Net realizable value

May be less than cost where selling prices have fallen or there is obsolescence, deterioration, or faulty production and the cost of rectification would take total costs above selling price, and where there is a decision to sell a product at a loss.

If the realizable value of raw materials have fallen below purchase price, there is no need to reduce them to NRV if they are to be incorporated into products which can be sold at a profit after accounting for the materials at cost price.

Cross-references

CA 1985
(i) Formats require disclosure under four headings, i.e raw materials, work in progress, finished goods, and payments on account. (ii) Methods allowed for determining purchase price or production cost include LIFO. (iii) Stock must not exceed purchase or production cost. Purchase price is stated as including 'any consideration (whether in cash or otherwise) given by the company . . .' Counsel's opinion indicates that this has been included so that debtors may be stated at face value (i.e. including the profit element). (iv) Replacement values to be disclosed by way of note if materially different to historic cost. (v) Stocks may be included at 'current cost' if the alternative accounting rules are adopted.

Standards
IAS 2 accords fairly closely to this part of SSAP 9 but with change of emphasis. Requirement to use FIFO or weighted average more positive but then LIFO and base stock permitted providing additional disclosure of difference between carrying value and either (a) value using FIFO etc. or (b) current cost. Fixed production overheads should be included but may be excluded if considered not directly related to bringing stock to location and condition, and that fact disclosed.

Interesting points

Semantics
The original SSAP resorted to placing the words 'actual cost' in quote marks, presumably recognising an ambiguity since 'actual cost' can only be arrived at by the exercise of judgement. The revised SSAP makes less use of the word 'actual' and simply refers to cost.

Principles
Accruals (matching) is the fundamental concept which requires the cost of unsold stock to be carried forward, prudence for write down to net realizable value. Matching also justifies including fixed production overheads but prudence would require a write-off in the period. The ASC has preferred matching to prudence for these period costs.

Problems
Management might prefer costing records on a 'marginal cost' basis as the information this produces is more helpful. Compliance with SSAP 9 can be achieved by a 'one-off' adjustment for fixed overheads at the year end.

Illustrations

1)   The individual line basis:

	Net realizable value	Cost
Stock items – category A	14,000	10,000
Stock items – category B	12,000	13,000
Stock items – category C	16,000	10,000
Totals	42,000	33,000

In total, the cost of £33,000 is lower but valuation must be based on figures for each category of stock. Valuation would therefore be:

	Lower
Stock items – category A	10,000
Stock items – category B	12,000
Stock items – category C	10,000
	32,000

2)   Using definition of net realizable value:

An item of stock cost £1,000. It has been damaged and as it stands it could be sold for £600. The company intends to repair it at a cost of £100 so that it can be sold for £900.

Net realizable value is:

Eventual selling price	900
Less cost to complete	100
	800

This is lower than cost and will be the basis of the valuation. By bringing this into the accounts as closing stock the ultimate loss of £200 is recognised immediately. The ultimate loss of £200 will be sales revenue of £900 less total costs of (1,000 + 100) £1,100.

3)   Firm sales order:

A company had purchased raw materials costing £10,000 to be incorporated into a product for a customer who had contracted to pay £20,000 for the finished product. The conversion costs will be £6,000 but work has not been started. At the balance sheet the market price for the raw materials on hand had dropped to £8,000.

The raw materials can be valued at cost of £10,000 since the net realizable value will be taken as (20,000 – 6,000) £14,000

4)   Normal course of business. Cost of being inefficient in current period should not be carried forward in stock. Examples:

(a) Materials: Raw materials consumed was £48,000 but this included £4,000 for abnormal spoilage. The amount which should be charged to finished goods is £44,000.

(b) Overheads: Fixed overheads attributable to production £100,000. Normal capacity is 100,000 units but due to abnormal breakdowns only 80,000 units were produced. Unit overhead costs of finished goods must still be £1 per unit and the £20,000 under-absorbed must be written off.

Notes

Notes

SSAP 9 Stocks and work in progress – long-term contracts

Revised September 1988

Background

Business and accounting

An international survey published in 1968 (International Study Group) found that many construction companies in UK, USA, and Canada, were accounting for partial profits prior to completing a contract, although some preferred to wait until the contract was completed. SSAP 9 established a 'percentage of completion' method as standard practice in UK from 1975.

The original SSAP was written prior to the Companies Act 1981 (now 1985) and included requirements which were found to be in conflict with the new legislation. Two main problems arose:

1) the original SSAP required work in progress on long-term contracts to be carried in the balance sheet as a cumulative figure for 'costs to date plus attributable profit less foreseeable losses'. This basis was thought to contravene the legal requirement that stocks should not be carried in excess of cost.

2) the first item in a published profit and loss account prior to the 1981 Act was 'profit before tax', thereby allowing 'attributable profit' to be included as a single amount within this item. The 1981 Act introduced Formats which required disclosure of both turnover and cost of sales, and there was lack of agreement as to how the old SSAP should be articulated with these new requirements.

Developing the standard

Points considered

Reported results would be erratic if profit recognition is deferred until the contract is completed. The 'completed contracts method' does not give a fair view of contract activity during year.

Basic approach and method

Where the outcome is reasonably certain, recognize part of eventual profit before completion. If a loss is foreseeable, a provision for the whole loss should be made immediately.

A proportion of estimated total profit should be recognized as contract activity progresses. Profit attributable to work performed should be reflected in the profit and loss account by making periodic transfers of:

1) contract turnover;
2) the costs related to that turnover.

As regards costs, the carrying values for work in progress will no longer be cumulative but will represent costs incurred to date net of amounts transferred to profit and loss account (less, in some cases, a provision for foreseeable losses).

Cumulative turnover should be compared with total payments on account. If turnover exceeds payments on account, the balance should be treated as a debtor. If payments on account exceed turnover, the excess should be set against 'net cost' for that particular contract. Where payments on account exceed net cost, the residual balance should be treated as a creditor.

Definitions

Long-term contract
The manufacture or building of a single substantial asset (or provision of service) where the time taken to substantially complete the contract falls into different accounting periods.

Cost
See stocks and work in progress generally. Interest payments should be excluded unless they relate specifically to particular contract.

Attributable profit
Part of the currently estimated total profit that fairly reflects the profit attributable to work performed at the accounting date. When estimating eventual profit, make allowances for estimated remedial and maintenance costs and for any cost increases not recoverable under the terms of the contract. There should be no attributable profit until outcome of contract is reasonably certain.

Foreseeable losses
Those currently estimated to arise over the duration of the contract. Must be estimated irrespective of stage of contract (even if work has not been started) and irrespective of profits on other contracts.

Payments on account
Progress payments received and receivable.

The standard

Profit and loss account
Assess each contract on an individual basis. Reflect attributable profit

by recording turnover and related costs as contract activity progresses. Turnover ascertained in a manner appropriate to the stage of completion and practices within the relevant industry. Prudently calculated attributable profit to be recognised in the profit and loss account as the difference between reported turnover and related costs.

Balance sheet items

Various balances arise depending on the circumstances for each contract.

Contract costs will be net of amounts transferred to cost of sales. In some cases, a provision for foreseeable losses will be deducted from contract costs and charged to cost of sales. The resulting balance is described as 'net cost less foreseeable losses'.

If a provision for foreseeable losses exceeds net cost, the balance should be included within 'provisions for liabilities and charges'.

Balances arise where turnover recognized exceeds, or is less than, payments on account (i.e. progress payments received and receivable).

If turnover recognized exceeds payments on account, the difference should be classified as 'amounts recoverable on contracts' and included under debtors.

If turnover recognized is less than payments on account the resulting credit balance should be described as 'applicable payments on account' and offset against net costs on that contract. Where these payments exceed net cost (less foreseeable losses) the residual balance should be classified as 'payments on account' and included under creditors.

The amount classified as 'long-term contract balances' to be included under stocks will be the net result of two figures for each contract as below:

1) net cost less foreseeable losses;
2) applicable payments on account.

A balance sheet note should disclose each of these figures separately.

Presentation and disclosure

Most points are covered by the prescriptive section of the standard. The accounting policy applied, particularly for ascertaining turnover and attributable profit, should be stated.

Cross references

CA 1985

There is no conflict over treating attributable profit as realized because Sch. 4 para. 91 defines realized as those 'in accordance with principles generally accepted. . .' Recording profit according to SSAP 9 is an accepted principle (see ED40). Furthermore, recognition of attributable profit is based on the concept of 'reasonable certainty' as to eventual outcome (see ASC Technical Release No. 481, 1982).

Standards

IAS 11 deals specifically with construction contracts and allows either the 'completed contracts' or 'percentage of completion' methods. Percentage of completion requires considerations similar to SSAP 9. Both IAS 11 and SSAP 9 now define long-term contracts in much the same way (the previous SSAP 9 defined a long-term contract as one which exceeded 12 months). IAS 11 suggests that retentions are treated as debtors – these âre not mentioned in SSAP 9, although 'amounts recoverable on contracts' will, in many cases, include retention amounts.

Interesting points

Semantics

Turnover is not defined in either the SSAP or the Companies Act. Guidance in Appendix 1 of the SSAP suggests that turnover could be ascertained by reference to valuation of work to date. In other cases there may be specific stages at which individual elements of work done can be separately identified in terms of their sales value and related costs (para. 69). Also, see below under 'principles and problems'.

The term 'payments on account' is unfortunate. It gives the impression of cash payments (receipts to the contractor), yet it is defined as progress payments received and receivable (i.e. including progress payments earned but not yet received). This definition is not really appropriate for the balance sheet item because the credit balance concerned relates to progress payments earned but not yet recognized as turnover.

Principles and problems

Attributable profit: in most cases the first step each year will be to calculate attributable profit. A basis must then be decided for determining turnover and related costs in order to reflect this profit in the financial statements.

The standard (and guidance notes) require attributable profit to be calculated as a proportion of the total estimated profit, but no method (or guidance) is given for measuring this proportion. Presumably it could be based on the proportion of cost completed, or proportion of sales value completed. The international survey (see 'Background') stated that most policies were based on the proportion of cost completed. IAS 11 mentions proportion of cost completed as possible basis.

Determining attributable profit by comparing value of work certified with cost of work certified does not appear to be acceptable since it ignores activities beyond the current stage of completion – but see below regarding contracts which are delivered in discrete stages.

Turnover: there appear to be at least two bases that could be applied (in exams, if not in practice), namely:

1) cost of work certified plus attributable profit;

2) Value of work certified (in which case, cost of sales will be the value of work certified less attributable profit).

The guidance notes (and Appendix 3) suggest that even if no profit is to be recognized (e.g. in the early stages of a contract) it may be appropriate to reflect turnover and costs in the profit and loss account by using a figure of zero for attributable profit.

   In some businesses, contracts are performed in discrete stages for which prices are separately agreed. In these cases, costs could be matched with the revenues earned for completing the separable part of the contract. Consideration must still be given to future costs and revenues for the whole contract, and provisions made for any foreseeable losses.

Prudence: is best exercised by taking a prudent view of future costs and commitments when estimating ultimate profit. This ensures that attributable profit is also calculated on a prudent basis. The idea that prudence should be exercised by applying some kind of arbitrary fraction to attributable profit (as suggested in some texts) has no conceptual basis or merit.

Illustrations

The following information relates to five contracts that were in progress at the accounting date.

Contract	A	B	C	D	E
Contract price	4 000	10 000	5 000	8 000	8 000
Costs incurred to date	2 400	1 500	380	7 000	200
Estimated future costs	498	8 548	4 728	312	5 800
Certified value of work done	2 800	1 650	336	7 700	210
Cost of work certified	1 840	1 390	336	6 800	200
Progress payments invoiced	2 230	1 480	300	6 600	189
Progress payments received	2 100	1 480	300	6 600	189
Estimated total costs	2 898	10 048	5 108	7 312	6 000
Estimated total profit/(loss)	1 102	(48)	(108)	688	2 000

The accounting policy is to recognize attributable profit as a proportion of total estimated profit, based on the proportion of total estimated costs which have been incurred and valued up to the accounting date. No profit is to be recognized on contract E since it is not sufficiently advanced in order to predict its eventual outcome. Turnover is based on cost of work certified plus attributable profit.

Calculations will therefore show:

Contract	A	B	C	D	E
Attributable profit	700			640	0
Foreseeable loss		(48)	(108)		

The profit and loss account will include:

	A	B	C	D	E
Turnover	2 540	1 390	336	7 440	200
Cost of sales:					
contract costs	1 840	1 390	336	6 800	200
provision for losses		48	108		
total	1 840	1 438	444	6 800	200
Profit/(loss)	700	(48)	(108)	640	0

Workings for the balance sheet:

	A	B	C	D	E
Net cost	560	110	44	200	0
Less provision for losses		(48)	(108)		
Net cost less provision	560	62	0	200	0
Applicable payments on account		(90)			
Set off against net cost		62			

Balance sheet will therefore include:

	A	B	C	D	E
Under stocks:					
Long-term contract balances	560	0	0	200	0
Under debtors:					
Amounts recoverable on contracts	310		36	840	11
Debtor for progress payments due	130				
Under creditors:					
Payments on account		(28)			
Under provision for liabilities and charges:					
Provision for future losses		(64)			

Note: An interesting situation would arise on contract D if turnover is based on the value of work certified of £7,700. If an attributable profit of £640 is to be recognized it would be necessary to transfer contract costs of (7,700 − 640) £7,060 to cost of sales, and yet costs incurred to date are only £7,000. A credit balance of £60 would arise on the contract account – what is this? A negative net cost or an accrual?

Notes

SSAP 10 Statements of source and application of funds

Issued July 75

Background

Business
Accounts usually presented minimum information required by law.

Accounting
Funds statement had been used voluntarily for very many years as a means of explaining movements in financial position between two dates.

Users
Often misunderstand profit and have difficulty in relating it to changes in financial position during a period.

Law
No statutory requirement.

Developing the standard

Points considered
Profit and loss account alone does not provide sufficient link between opening and closing balances for a full understanding of changes in the companies financial position.

Basic approach and method
Funds statement would help identify movements by summarising and re-classifying information from existing statements. Audited accounts to include additional funds statement if turnover is £25,000 or more with voluntary disclosure if under. Objective is to show how operations are financed and how resources have been used.

Definitions

Net liquid funds
Cash, cash equivalents (e.g. current asset investments) less overdrafts and borrowings repayable within one year.

The standard

Applicable
All financial accounts intended to give true and fair view except where turnover is below £25,000.

Requirements
Include statement of source and application of funds for current and previous period.

Presentation and disclosure

Contents
Operating profit and adjustments for items not involving movement of funds; dividends paid; fixed assets acquired and disposed; cash flows through changes in loan capital (long and medium term) and issued capital; increases and decreases in working capital sub-divided into its component parts; and movements in net liquid funds.

Guidance
Minimum of netting off. Figures generally identifiable with those in the profit and loss account and balance sheet.

Groups
Base on group accounts. The purchase or disposal of subsidiaries may be reflected as (a) single item, or (b) part of the movements on relevant assets and liabilities. Summarize in a footnote, including details of consideration given if an acquisition.

Cross-references

Standards
References to financial statements in other SSAPs include the funds statement. IAS 7 discusses various practices but prescribes very few rules, e.g. it notes that in some cases no adjustment is made for profits of associates and so the increase in equity value of the investment is treated as an application.

Interesting points

Semantics
The word 'funds' escapes definition and is used in a working capital (accruals) context so that profit can be included in the statement as one of the sources and linked (together with other sources and applications) to the changes in working capital. IAS 7 mentions: cash, cash equivalents or working capital.

Principles
Standard insists on strict cash flow basis for dividends but not for any other profit items. Normal practice is to deal with tax and sale of assets on strict cash flow basis.

Problems
Although mandatory for companies with turnover of £25,000 or more the statement is probably of more help to smaller businesses where contents are simple and easily understood. Statements for complex groups tend to include items which are difficult for a non-accountant user to appreciate.

Footnotes on group problems:
1)   Minority interests and profits retained in associated company:

Examples given in the Appendix to SSAP 10 start off with: profit before tax less minority interests.This then involves making adjustments for:

a)   minority interest in retained profits for year – added since it is a source which partly funds the increase in group net assets;
b)   profits retained in associate company – deducted since these funds have not been received and the increase in carrying value of investment is not treated as an application (see notes above on IAS 7 for possible alternative).

An alternative would be to start off with profit before tax excluding the share of associated company's profit and to make no adjustment for minority interests. Dividends received from associates are then added as a source, and dividends to minority interests are an application. Either basis produces figures which are not immediately apparent from the accounts. See example in this guide for dividend basis.

2)   Subsidiary acquired during year:

Examples given in the Appendix to SSAP 10 are based on the following acquisition:

Net assets acquired:		Discharged by:	
Fixed assets	290	Share issue	290
Goodwill	30	Cash	60
Stocks	40		
Debtors	30		
Creditors	(40)		
	350		350

This is presented in one example as a single application of £350 and in another the separate assets and liabilities 'acquired' are included with the relevant movements of similar items. In both cases the above statement is given as a footnote and in both cases the share issue of £290 needs to be shown as a source. When the single item basis is used the figures are not immediately identifiable with the balance sheets, but can be found through the footnote.

Illustration

EFFECT OF MINORITY INTERESTS AND ASSOCIATED COMPANIES

Details

Outline consolidated profit		
Group profit before tax		40,000
Share of associated company's results		4,000
		44,000
Taxation: Group	16,000	
Associated company	1,000	17,000
Group profit after tax		27,000
Minority interests (20%)		2,000
		25,000
Dividends paid		5,000
Retained		20,000

Outline consolidated balance sheet:		
	Beginning	End
Fixed assets	100,000	102,000
Investment in associated company	60,000	62,000
Taxation creditor	(14,000)	(16,000)
Net current assets	110,000	128,000
Net liquid funds	4,000	5,000
	260,000	281,000
Share capital	100,000	100,000
Reserves	120,000	140,000
Minority interests	40,000	41,000
	260,000	281,000

Statement of retained profits:

	Group	Holding company	Subsidiary	Associated company
Brought forward	120,000	100,000	16,000	4,000
Retained for year	20,000	14,000	4,000	2,000
Carried forward	140,000	114,000	20,000	6,000

Depreciation charged during the year was £3,000 and there were no sales of fixed assets.

Outline statement of source and application of funds – using the dividend basis

Group profit before tax		40,000
Add dividend received from associated company		1,000
		41,000
Adjustments for items not involving movement of funds – depreciation		3,000
		44,000
Applications:		
Purchase of fixed assets	5,000	
Dividends paid – holding company	5,000	
– minority interests	1,000	
Taxation paid	14,000	
		25,000
		19,000
Represented by:		
Increase in net current assets		18,000
Increase in net liquid funds		1,000
		19,000

Workings
Dividend received from associated company – profits after tax
(4,000 − 1,000) = 3,000 less retained in associate 2,000. Dividends paid
to minority interests – Opening balance 40,000 add share of profits
2,000, less closing balance 41,000 = 1,000 paid. Purchase of fixed assets
102,000 − (100,000 − 3,000) = 5,000. Taxation paid = 14,000 + 16,000
− 16,000.

Notes

SSAP 12   Accounting for depreciation

Issued December 1977, amended November 1981, revised January 1987

Background

Business
Basis often arbitrary. SSAP 2 introduced some discipline although assets increasing in value (e.g. freehold property) not usually depreciated.

Accounting
Concepts debated by academics but profession adopted a pragmatic approach. The original SSAP 12 left many questions unresolved, particularly in relation to revalued assets. Refinements hampered through lack of agreement on inflation accounting.

Law
No legal requirement to depreciate fixed assets until CA 1981 – often cited as the reason for introducing original SSAP 12.

Developing the standard

Points considered
Most fixed assets have a finite life therefore the matching concept requires their cost to be allocated to the accounting periods which benefit from the use of such assets. This periodic charge is usually called depreciation. The matching concept would require depreciation even if market value exceeds book value.

Basic approach and method
Depreciate all assets which have a finite life (some exceptions) so that a fair proportion of the cost or valuation of the asset is charged to each period expected to benefit from its use. There are many acceptable methods and management must select the most appropriate.

Definitions

Depreciation
The measure of wearing out, consumption, other reduction in useful economic life of a fixed asset, whether through use, effluxion of time, or obsolescence through technological changes.

Useful economic life
Period over which the PRESENT OWNER will derive economic benefits.

Residual value
Realizable value at end of useful economic life (UEL) based on prices prevailing at time of acquisition or revaluation.

Recoverable amount
Greater of net realizable value and amount recoverable from further use.

The standard

Exceptions
Investment properties (SSAP 19); Goodwill (SSAP 22); Development costs (SSAP 13); Investments.

Provision
For fixed assets having a finite UEL should be made by allocating cost (or revalued amount) less estimated residual value, fairly to the periods expected to benefit from use of the asset. Methods chosen should be the most appropriate for the type of asset and its use.

Articulation
Treatment in the profit and loss account should be consistent with that used in the balance sheet. Hence the charge should be based on the asset's carrying value, historic cost or revalued amount. The whole charge should be made to the profit and loss account and none set 'directly' against reserves. Supplementary depreciation, i.e. that in excess of charge based on carrying amount, should not be charged to profit and loss account. This does not preclude appropriations to reserve for increased cost of replacing assets.

Asset lives
Estimate on a realistic basis, review regularly and revise when necessary. Regular review and revision of asset lives would usually not cause any material distortion of future results if net book value is written off over revised remaining UEL. If material distortions are likely the adjustments to accumulated depreciation should be dealt with per SSAP 6, i.e. usually as an ordinary item for the year.

Permanent diminution in value
If net book amount is not recoverable in full it should be written down

immediately to recoverable amount and then written off over remaining UEL. If the conditions cease to apply write back as no longer necessary. Provisions for diminution in value (and reversals) should be dealt with in the profit and loss account if they relate to an asset not previously revalued. Treatment where asset previously revalued has not been resolved by the standard.

Change of method
Permissible only on grounds of a fairer presentation. Such change does not constitute a change of policy and the net book amount should be written off over remaining UEL commencing in current period.

Revaluations
Base charge on revalued amount and remaining UEL. Depreciation previously charged not written back to profit unless relates to provisions for permanent diminution in value found unnecessary (as above). Valuations must be kept up to date.

Freehold property
Provision not normally required for land unless subject to depletion (e.g. mineral extraction). Land may require write down if subject to adverse conditions affecting value. Buildings no different to other assets in that they have a finite UEL, albeit significantly longer.

Disclosure

Each class of asset
Methods; UEL or depreciation rates; total charge; gross amounts of depreciable assets and related accumulated depreciation.

Change of basis
Effect if material and reasons.

Revaluations
Effect, if material, on charge for year of revaluation.

Cross-references

CA 1985
Some disclosure requirements additional to SSAP 12, e.g. where assets are revalued the depreciation based on revalued amount must be compared to that based on historic cost. Revaluations are permitted under 'alternative accounting rules'. If assets are revalued the difference between the value and depreciated historic cost must be taken to a revaluation reserve. This prevents a former practice of writing past depreciation provisions back to profit as no longer required and supports the requirements of SSAP 12 in this respect.

Standards
(i) SSAP 6 for change of policy. (ii) SSAP 15 for deferred tax on

revaluation surpluses. (iii) IAS 4 deals with depreciation and accords closely to SSAP 12 as far as it goes. Revaluations are dealt with in IAS 16 'accounting for property, plant and equipment'. There is no equivalent SSAP to IAS 16. Some provisions in IAS 16 are covered by CA 1985 and some by SSAP 12. It opposes selective revaluations of assets and prescribes for revaluation of an entire class or failing that selections to be made on a systematic basis. See also notes below dealing with sale of revalued assets.

Interesting points

Semantics
The original definition of depreciation has been slightly changed by the revised SSAP 12 as follows:

original: 'the measure of . . . or other loss in value'.
revised: 'the measure of . . . or other reduction in useful economic life'.

It could be that the word depreciation is given too much to do. It relates to the total loss in value between acquisition and disposal as well as the annual allocation of this total charged to profit. Perhaps defining depreciation as a measure of loss in value suggested that accountants measured the annual loss in value whereas the procedure is to allocate a fair slice of the total. The new definition is also more compatible with the requirement to depreciate assets which have a finite economic life, even though they may be gaining in value.

Principles
ASC seem to have taken strict theoretical line in two respects:

1) the cost of all assets with a finite UEL will be matched with income over the life of the asset although pressure from investment property companies yielded one exception (see SSAP 19);
2) if historic cost accounts are modified by revaluation of certain assets a current cost basis for depreciation on revalued assets is required. 'Split depreciation' (i.e. historic cost depreciation to profit and depreciation on revaluation surplus to revaluation reserve) is not permitted.

Problems
ED 36 which preceded the revised SSAP 6 intended to codify practice on sale of assets previously revalued. ED 37 which preceded the revised SSAP 12 referred to ED 36 in this respect but no mention of the suggested practice appears in either standard. An earlier attempt to deal with the problem was made by ED 16 but it was never converted into a standard. The ED 16 basis was different to that in ED 36. The two methods can be summarized as follows:

	Gain or loss determined by comparing sale proceeds to:	Effect on past revaluation surpluses:
ED 36	depreciated original cost	transfer to profit and loss
ED 16	net carrying value	remain on reserve.

Both methods are permitted under the CA 1985. They are illustrated below. IAS 16 requires profits or losses to be determined by comparing sale proceeds to net carrying value but there is an explanatory note which states that past revaluation surpluses 'may' then be transferred to retained earnings.

Illustrations

1) SALE OF PREVIOUSLY REVALUED ASSET

Cost of asset with 10 year life £10,000. During 4th year revalued to £14,000 and remaining UEL of 7 years not changed. During 6th year sold for £10,600

			Revaluation reserve	
	ED 36 basis	ED 16 basis	ED 36 basis	ED 16 basis
Cost	10,000	10,000		
Depreciation 3 years	3,000	3,000		
	7,000	7,000		
Revaluation surplus	7,000	7,000	7,000	7,000
	14,000	14,000		
Depreciation 2 years	4,000	4,000		
WDV on sale	10,000	10,000		
Sale proceeds	10,600	10,600		
Difference	600	600		
Revaluation reserve released	7,000	—	(7,000)	
Profit reported	7,600	600	—	7,000

Reconciliation of reported profit under ED 36 basis:

Original cost	£10,000
Depreciation charged	7,000
Depreciated original cost	3,000
Sale proceeds	10,600
Profit reported	7,600

Effect on profit over whole period:

	ED 36	ED 16
Depreciation charged	7,000	7,000
Profit on sale credited	(7,600)	(600)
Net	Gain 600	Loss 6,400

ED 36 results in a net credit to profit for the capital gain of

(£10,600 − £10,000) £600 and therefore, over the course of time, both historic cost and sale proceeds have been dealt with through profit and loss account. The net debit to profit under ED 16 represents only a part of historic cost – the remaining £3,600 and the sale proceeds of £10,600 are represented by a separate reserve (now realized) of £7,000.

2) REVISION OF ASSET LIVES

(a) Asset cost £30,000 originally estimated to have a 20 year life. After 5 years at this rate it is estimated that the remaining UEL is only 10 years.

Comment: There is not likely to be any material distortions to future profits if the residue of cost is simply written off over remaining UEL: Residue of cost £30,000 − (5 × £1,500) = £22,500. Future depreciation £2,250 per annum compared to £2,000 per annum if past provisions were adjusted to recognize revised estimate of UEL.

(b) Asset costing £150,000 originally estimated to have a 50 year life. After 5 years at this rate it is estimated that the remaining UEL is only 5 years.

Comment: If residue of cost (£150,000 − £15,000) £135,000 is written off over remaining UEL future charges would be £27,000 per annum. If existing provision is adjusted to recognize revised estimate of UEL the company should have provided (5 × £15,000) £75,000 leaving future charges to be £15,000 per annum. If the company decided to make an adjustment in the current year for the £60,000 previously under-provided it must be treated as an ordinary (perhaps exceptional) item and not as a prior year adjustment.

Notes

SSAP 13 Accounting for research and development

Issued October 1977, revised January 1989

Background

Business

Advances in technology led to increased expenditure on research and development particularly in the electronics and aircraft industry. It was claimed that expenditure created an intangible asset producing future benefits.

Accounting

Conflicting views were expressed between prudence and matching. Original exposure draft (ED14) saw the relationship between expenditure and future benefits as being too uncertain and favoured immediate write-off on the grounds of prudence. After representations from aerospace industry ED17 issued which required deferral of development costs in some cases. The requirement to defer was derogated to one of allowing deferral in the final SSAP. A few minor changes were made to the SSAP in January 1989, the main one being to require disclosure of the amounts charged as expenses in the profit and loss account (not required in the original).

Developing the standard

Points considered

Prudence requires an expense to be written off unless its relationship to future revenue can be established. Definitions, particularly the distinction between research and development, to be based on those provided by the Organisation for Economic Co-operation and Development (OECD).

Basic approach and method

Pure and applied research are part of continuing process and as no one particular period is expected to benefit all research costs should be written off as incurred. The development of new or improved products is usually undertaken with the expectation of future benefits, either through increased revenue or reduced costs, therefore deferral allowed where potential benefits can be evaluated.

Definitions

Research costs
Divided between pure research and applied research as follows:

Pure
Original investigation to gain new scientific or technical knowledge, not primarily directed towards specific practical aim or application.

Applied
Original investigation to gain new scientific or technical knowledge which is directed towards specific practical aim or objective.

Development costs
Use of scientific and technical knowledge to produce new or substantially improved: materials, devices, products, processes, systems, or services, prior to commencing commercial production.

Exclusions
Mineral exploitation. Research and development undertaken for third parties where terms of contract provide reimbursement of expenditure, should be treated as work in progress until reimbursed.

The standard

Fixed assets
Those which provide facilities for research and development should be capitalized and written off over useful life.

Research
Pure and applied (except fixed assets) write off as incurred.

Development
Written off as incurred but deferral permitted if:

1) clearly defined project;
2) expenditure separately identifiable;
3) outcome assessed with reasonable certainty as to technical feasibility and commercial viability;
4) future revenues reasonably expected to cover aggregate of all development costs on project;
5) adequate resources exist (reasonably expected to be available) to complete project.

Amortization
Commence with commercial production, allocate on a systematic basis by reference to sales or use, or periods over which expected to be sold or used. Once written off cannot be reinstated even if circumstances change.

Review
At end of each period and if circumstances which justified deferral no

longer apply, or are considered doubtful, write off to extent irrecoverable.

Consistency
If deferral policy is chosen it must be applied to all qualifying projects (revised SSAP).

Presentation and disclosure

Accounting policy. Balance separately in balance sheet. Movements. Disclose amounts charged to profit and loss, analysed between current year's expenditure and amounts amortized.

Cross references

CA 1985
Requires all research costs to be written off as incurred. Development costs may be capitalized in 'special circumstances', which are not defined but presumably per SSAP 13. Disclose write-off period and reasons for capitalization. Formats prescribe manner of presentation.

Standards
(i) SSAP 2 basic concepts (ii) SSAP 15 deferred tax on timing differences. (iii) SSAP 13, as revised, is now consistent with IAS 9.

Interesting points

Semantics
Distinction between the two types of research may seem pointless since both written off. Maybe it provides a helpful demarcation point on which to judge where research finishes and development starts.

Principles
(i) Depreciation of fixed assets included in research and development costs must also be included in the disclosure of depreciation. (ii) Market research is not within OECD definition but treat same as other research costs except where it relates to assessing market viability of a product for which costs are deferred – it may then be carried forward and disclosed separately.

Problems
Decisions on capitalization centre on various elements of uncertainty. Judgments at many different levels are required, e.g. marketing, production, finance. Viewing the uncertainties in light of prudence suggests that most costs would have to be written off. Book-keeping problems include classifying costs between research and development and in coding development expense between various projects.

Illustration

The following details relate to four projects.

	Project W	Project X	Project Y	Project Z
Deferred development costs b/fwd	80,000	25,000		
Costs in period:				
Wages	4,000		25,000	16,000
Expense	1,000		3,000	2,000
Depreciation	2,000		1,000	2,000
Balance at end of year	87,000	25,000	29,000	20,000

Project W
Position: Development has been completed, production and sales commenced. The marketing department estimate that 5,000 units per annum will be sold over the next two years. After this the product will start to become obsolete and will have to be replaced by an improved version. Selling price is £600 per unit and manufacturing cost £400 per unit.

Comment: The project appears to be commercially viable and the forecast profits of £2,000,000 more than cover the development costs. The expenditure may therefore be deferred and amortized on a systematic basis. The amortization basis could be either the time period of two years or on a unit basis of £8.70 per unit sold. The write off should commence in current year.

Project X
Position: The commercial production of this product commenced two years ago and was expected to run for at least five years. During the current year sales had dropped to a very low level and production ceased.

Comment: As the circumstances which justified deferral no longer apply the expenditure must be written off.

Project Y
Position: The company has been experimenting with some new microelectronics and has solved most of the basic problems. It is still working on how to apply the knowledge gained so that it can be incorporated into a marketable product.

Comment: In the absence of further details this would appear to be applied research and should be written off.

Project Z
Position: This work is being carried out under contract for a creditworthy client and is very much in the early stages of experimentation.

Comment: This may be treated as work in progress. In appropriate circumstances it may be classed as a long-term contract and subject to SSAP 9

Note: The disclosure of depreciation in the published accounts must include the £5,000 charged to these projects.

Notes

SSAP 14   Group accounts

Issued September 1978

Background

Business
Acquiring a controlling interest in another company rather than acquiring its net assets had become a convenient form of business combination. Group structures also provide a means of dividing a complex business into decentralised managerial units.

Accounting
Practice of presenting consolidated accounts grew up piecemeal and established over many years. There was no legal requirement to present group accounts until CA 1948 although stock exchange regulations had required them from 1939. Under CA 1948 group accounts were allowed to be in form other than consolidated accounts. An IAS (IAS 3) had been issued prior to SSAP 14.

Definitions
Subsidiary
Defined from the standpoint of holding company, i.e. a company is a subsidiary of another if that other company:
is member of it and controls its board of directors;
or holds more than half the nominal value of its equity share capital;
or (to encompass indirect subsidiaries) the subsidiary itself is subsidiary of any company which is a subsidiary of that other company.

Holding company
One that has a subsidiary.

Group
A holding company and its subsidiaries.

Financial statements
Balance sheets, profit and loss accounts, statements of source and application funds, other statements which collectively give a true and fair view of results and financial position.

Group accounts
Financial statements of a group.

Consolidated financial statements
One form of group accounts which presents the information included in the separate financial statements of holding company and subsidiaries as if they were financial statements of a single entity.

Equity share capital
Issued capital excluding that part which only carries a right to participate in distributions (capital or dividends) up to a specified amount.

Equity method of accounting
Where an investment is shown in the consolidated balance sheet at cost plus the investor's share of post acquisition profits retained by investee (less amounts written off) and the consolidated profit and loss account includes the investor's share of investee's profit for the year. This method is normally applied to associated companies under SSAP 1.

The standard

Group accounts
Must be in the form of consolidated financial statements. The only exceptions are those prescribed in the standard. A description of bases used to incorporate subsidiaries should be given.

The standard – other matters

Uniform policies
Should be followed throughout the group. If not adopted in subsidiary appropriate adjustments must be made in the group accounts. Where uniformity is not practicable different policies may be used providing they are generally acceptable and following disclosed: the different policies, the reasons for using them, items involved and the effect on results and net assets.

Accounting periods
Wherever practicable financial statements of subsidiary should be to same date and for same period as holding company. Where dates are not identical (and impracticable to prepare special accounts for consolidation) adjustments should be made for any abnormal transactions in the intervening period. Disclose: subsidiary's name; accounting date; reasons for using different date (DTI consent is required).

Exclusions
Consolidated accounts are not required if the holding company is a wholly owned subsidiary of another company. A subsidiary may be excluded from consolidation in the following cases:

Dissimilar activities: so dissimilar that consolidated accounts would be misleading and users needs better satisfied by presenting separate accounts.

Lack of effective control: holding company owns more than half the equity but does not own more than half the voting capital or (for contractual or other reasons) is unable to appoint a majority to the board.

Severe restrictions: of control by the holding company of the subsidiary's operations for foreseeable future.
Control is intended to be *temporary.*

Accounting for subsidiaries excluded
Depends on reasons for exclusion, namely:

Dissimilar activities: include separate financial statements (combined with others if appropriate). Disclose: interest; inter-group balances; nature of transactions with group; reconciliation with amounts included in consolidated financial statements which should be dealt with under the equity method.

Lack of effective control: equity method if it satisfies other criteria for associated companies per SSAP 1, otherwise investment at cost (or valuation) less any provisions required. In either case disclose the separate information required to satisfy CA requirements.

Severe restrictions: investment at the amount it would have been under equity method at date when restrictions came into force. There should be no further accruals of profit but where value of investment is impaired provide for the loss through consolidated profit. Disclose for each subsidiary: net assets; results for period; amounts included in consolidated profit for dividends and any amounts written off the investment.

Temporary control: include in consolidated balance sheet as current asset at lower of cost and net realizable value.

All cases: disclose: reasons; names; premium or discount on acquisition (by comparison to fair values of assets acquired); any information required by the Companies Act.

Minority interests
Balance sheet: as a separate item but not part of shareholders' funds. Debit balances should only be recognized when there is a binding obligation on the minority interests to make good the loss.

Share of profits: separate item after profit after tax before extraordinary items. Minority interests in extraordinary items to be deducted from related amounts.

Distribution restrictions
Where there are significant restrictions on ability of holding company to distribute retained group profits because of statutory, contractual, or exchange control restrictions (e.g. on a foreign subsidiary), state the extent of restrictions.

Disclosure
For each principal subsidiary: names; proportion of nominal value of each class held; nature of business.

Acquisitions and disposals

Effective date
Earlier of when consideration passes or when offer is declared unconditional. Applies even if agreement to share profits from earlier date.

Premium or discount on acquisition
Underlying net assets (excluding goodwill) at FAIR VALUE to the acquiring company compared with purchase consideration. Any difference is the premium or discount on acquisition. Where assets are not adjusted to fair value in subsidiary's books, memorandum adjustments must be made for consolidation.

Profit and losses of subsidiary
Sufficient information to enable shareholders to appreciate the effect on consolidated results for the year.

Disposals
Consolidated profit and loss account to include subsidiary's results up to date of disposal, and any gain or loss on sale of the investment found by taking the difference between sale proceeds and share net assets at date of disposal together with premium or discount on acquisition.

Cross-references

CA 1985
Schedule 4A, introduced by the 1989 Companies Act, deals with the form and content of group accounts. The 1989 Act introduces new definitions for parent and subsidiary that conflict with those in the current SSAP. Acquisition accounting must be used unless conditions for merger accounting are met (see SSAP 23). Small and medium groups are exempted from the requirement to prepare group accounts. These 1989 amendments stem from adoption of the EC 7th Directive.

Standards
(i) SSAP 23 states that SSAP 14 does not prescribe for acquisition accounting except under 'acquisitions and disposals'. (ii) Both SSAP 22 and 23 deal with goodwill arising on consolidation. (iii) Gain or loss on disposal of a subsidiary must be dealt with according to SSAP 6.

Interesting points

Principles
Consolidated accounts are an amalgam of different value bases. The

subsidiary's assets at time when control was acquired will be at fair values whilst its subsequent additions (and others in the group) will be at purchase cost less depreciation. Goodwill arising on consolidation only represents the holding company's share of its value whilst other assets of subsidiary are carried in full with minority interests share shown separately.

Illustration

OUTLINE EXAMPLE – MECHANICS OF CONSOLIDATION UNDER ACQUISITION METHOD

Profit and loss accounts

	Hold Ltd	Sub Ltd
Turnover	10,000	8,000
Cost of sales and other expenses	6,000	4,000
Profit before tax	4,000	4,000
Taxation	1,000	2,000
Profit after tax	3,000	2,000
Proposed dividends	2,000	800
Retained for year	1,000	1,200

Statements of retained profit:

	Hold Ltd	Sub Ltd
Beginning of year	20,000	12,000
Retained for year	1,000	1,200
End of year	21,000	13,200

Balance sheets

	Hold Ltd	Sub Ltd
Tangible fixed assets	20,000	10,000
Investment in subsidiary (60% int)	10,000	—
Proposed dividends	(2,000)	(800)
Other net current assets	3,000	8,000
	31,000	17,200
Ordinary Shares of £1,00 each	10,000	4,000
Retained profits	21,000	13,200
	31,000	17,200

Hold Ltd acquired its 60% interest in Sub Ltd when Sub's capital was £4,000 and reserves were £10,000, i.e. net assets £14,000 at book value; fair value to Hold Ltd = £15,000.

Calculations: Premium on acquisition £10,000 less (60% of £15,000) = £1,000.

Minority interests: Profits for year 40% of £2,000 = £800; Proposed div 40% of £800 = £320; Balance due to minority interests 40% of (£17,200 + Revaluation reserve of £1,000) = £7,280.

Tangible fixed assets 20,000 + 10,000 + 1,000 (Revaluation reserve) = £31,000.

Consolidated accounts:

	Profit & loss		*Balance sheet*
Turnover	18,000	Tangible fixed assets	31,000
Cost of sales and		Other net current	
other expense	10,000	assets	11,000
Profit before tax	8,000	Proposed divs – Hold	(2,000)
Taxation	3,000	– Sub (MI)	(320)
Profit after tax	5,000		39,680
Minority interests	800		
Profit for financial year	4,200	Share capital	10,000
Proposed divs	2,000	Consolidated reserves	23,400
Retained for year	2,200	Goodwill	(1,000)
		Minority interests	7,280
			39,680

Statement of retained profits

Beginning of year	21,200
Retained for year	2,200
End of year	23,400

Notes:

1) Profits for financial year (a) Dealt with in accounts Hold − £3,000 + dividend receivable of £480 = £3,480; (b) Retained in Sub – 60% of £1,200 = £720; Total £4,200.

2) Reserves carried forward: Hold £21,000 + £480 (div) = £21,480; Retained in Sub £1,920 i.e. 60% of Sub's post acquisition profits of £3,200 (£13,200 less £10,000);

Total carried forward (21,480 + 1,920) £23,400.

Notes

SSAP 15 Accounting for deferred taxation

Issued October 1978 (SSAP 11 withdrawn), revised May 1985

Background

Business

Differences between taxable profit and accounting profit are partly caused by items being included in taxable profit for a period which does not coincide with the period in which they are included for accounting. These timing differences usually have the effect of deferring tax to later periods. They were more noticeable following the introduction of certain tax reliefs which were granted to cushion the impact of taxation at a time when industry claimed their profits were being distorted by inflation.

SSAP 11 required a provision for deferred tax on all timing differences. This resulted in protests and non-compliance by industry. Compliance would have meant building up large deferred tax balances which might be regarded as debt by outsiders even when liabilities were not likely to crystallize e.g. where the company was continually investing in new fixed assets.

Accounting

The first standard took a strict arithmetical approach rather than allowing a reasoned assessment of the position. Developments in accounting for deferred tax show a constant change of thought as between the full provision and partial provision basis and between the deferral and liability methods.

Users

Earnings after tax are widely regarded as an indicator of performance and therefore the effect of timing differences on tax charges becomes significant.

Developing the standard

Points considered

There are three principal bases, namely:

nil provision or flow through where only the obligation to pay tax is recognized. It is based on the claim that tax on timing differences is difficult to quantify as it depends on the incidence of future events;

full provision or comprehensive allocation where the accounts recognize the tax effects of all item sin the period, both current and deferred;

partial provision which recognizes that a hard core of originating timing differences in a continuing business can create a permanent deferral.

The advantage of the first two bases is that they are both capable of precise quantification but certainty of calculation should not be given precedence over a reasoned assessment as required for the partial provision basis.

There are two principal methods of computation which require the effect of changes in tax rates to be considered, namely:

deferral method: based on the concept that there is a deferred credit which originates in one period in the form of increased income because of reduced taxes. This credit should be measured at the tax rate when it arose. Changes in tax rates are ignored since the credit does not represent an obligation to pay money.

liability method: based on the concept that a liability has been deferred to a period when the timing differences will reverse. The liability should be based on the rate of tax which is likely to apply on reversal.

Basic approach and method

Deferred tax only provided for timing differences expected to crystallize into liabilities. Partial provision based on reasonable assumptions. The original SSAP 15 allowed the provision to be based on either the liability or deferral methods. This was revised to liability only in 1985. The revised SSAP states that the liability method is consistent with the aim of partial provision, which is to provide for liabilities likely to crystallize.

Definitions

Timing differences

Differences between taxable profit and accounting profit which result from items of income and expenditure being dealt with in the tax computations for periods different from those in which included in financial statements. They originate in one period and are capable of reversal in one or more subsequent periods. A tax loss available to relieve future profits is a timing difference. A revaluation surplus is a timing difference if a subsequent realisation of the profit would become taxable – see guidance notes.

Liability method

Where deferred tax is calculated at a rate that is estimated will be applicable when timing differences reverse (long-term tax rate).

The standard

Deferred tax
Compute under liability method only to the extent it is probable that a liability (or asset) will crystallize. Use latest tax rate unless future rates known.

Crystallization assessment
Based on reasonable assumptions from information available to date accounts approved and the intentions of management. Consider financial plans and projections over sufficient years. Take a prudent view of any uncertainties.

Debit balances
Liabilities should be reduced by debit balances from separate categories of timing differences and by any ACT available for offset. Net debit balances not carried as assets unless expected recoverable.

Presentation and disclosure

PROFIT AND LOSS ACCOUNT

Deferred tax provided
On ordinary activities separately as part of tax charge (face or notes). On extraordinary separately as part of its own tax charge.

Adjustments
For changes in tax rates normally disclosed separately as part of tax charge. If from significant change of government fiscal policy (e.g. change of tax system) treat as extraordinary if material.

BALANCE SHEET AND NOTES

Disclose balance and movements. If from movements on reserves (e.g. relates to a revalued asset) show these transfers separately.

Not provided
Analyse into major categories and disclose amounts in a note. Calculations to be at long-term rate.

Revalued assets
If deferred tax not provided because revaluation does not constitute a timing difference such fact should be stated. Where values are only given in notes but they are materially different to book value, show the tax effects which would arise if assets were realized at noted value.

Guidance notes

Permanent differences
Will not reverse and have no effects on other periods. Examples

include disallowable expenses such as UK entertaining and non taxable credits such as regional development grants.

Crystallization of timing differences
Consider the combined effect rather than individual items when deciding if liability will crystallize. Projections may be for relatively short periods (3 to 5 years) where pattern regular.

Short term
Normally reverse in following period and usually arise through use of cash basis for tax and accruals basis for accounts, e.g. interest.

Other examples cash/accrual differences
Deferred development costs (allowed for tax when paid); pension costs accrued; provisions for repairs.

Both short term and other differences
Considered together when assessing if if liability will crystallize. Requirement in original SSAP 15 to provide for all short term timing differences no longer applies.

Capital allowances
Where accelerated capital allowances are of a recurring nature reversals may be offset (wholly/partly) by new originating differences thus allowing indefinite postponement. If irregular, consider a longer period.

Revaluations
Potential timing difference for tax payable when asset sold. May not crystallize if 'roll over relief' expected. Any provision should be made out of revaluation surplus. Where values not incorporated in accounts disclose the tax effect even if values are stated in directors' report instead of accounts.

Losses
Trading loss treated as recoverable if it results from an identifiable non-recurring cause and assurance beyond reasonable doubt that future profits will be sufficient to offset. *Capital loss* may be treated as recoverable if there is a decision to realize sufficient potential gain on other assets.

Cross references

CA 1985
(i) Balance sheet formats prescribe for disclosure of deferred tax liabilities and assets but no reference in profit and loss formats. (ii) Legal advice obtained by ASC states that any deferred tax not provided would be a 'contingent liability' except where prospect of becoming payable is remote.

Standards
IAS 12 is similar to SSAP 15 in many respects but allows either the

liability or deferral method to be used. The idea of providing tax on timing differences is referred to as the 'tax effect method'. This is compared to the 'tax payable method' where timing differences are ignored. The tax effect method is required (partial provision) and is justified by the accruals concept.

Interesting points

Principles
(i) Strange that original SSAP 15 allowed deferral method when the principle is to provide for possible liabilities. USA practice favours deferral method. (ii) Liability on reversal cannot be determined accurately since future rates of tax are not known. Explanatory notes comment that current rate is used as a best estimate. (iii) Accounting thought seems to have matured recently by giving more emphasis to assessing the view rather than finding arithmetical solutions. (iv) The withdrawal of stock relief and first year allowances may have reduced the impact of deferred tax problems.

Illustration

Timing differences caused by capital allowances:
 New plant cost £16,000 depreciated straight line over 16 years. Allowance for tax 25% on reducing balance. No further additions anticipated for next 10 years. Profits before depreciation £20,000 each year. Corporation tax is 50% for all years and there are no other timimg differences involved.
 If no provision made for deferred tax the reported profits for the first three years after purchase would be as follows:

	Year 1	Year 2	Year 3
Profit before depreciation	20,000	20,000	20,000
Depreciation	1,000	1,000	1,000
	19,000	19,000	19,000
Corporation tax (see below)	8,000	8,500	8,875
Profit after tax	11,000	10,500	10,125

Tax computations:

Profit per accounts	19,000	19,000	19,000
add: depreciation	1,000	1,000	1,000
	20,000	20,000	20,000
less: capital allowance	4,000	3,000	2,250
Taxable profit	16,000	17,000	17,750

Capital allowances are accelerating the plant write off for tax purposes (compared to accounting). In effect tax is being deferred to those periods when depreciation will be greater than capital allowances, i.e. from year 6 onwards in the example.

Calculations and adjustments for deferred tax are as follows:

Capital allowance	4,000	3,000	2,250
Depreciation	1,000	1,000	1,000
Originating timing difference	3,000	2,000	1,250
Tax on timing differences (50%)	1,500	1,000	625

Revised profit statements:

Profit before tax	19,000	19,000	19,000
Corporation Tax (as before)	(8,000)	(8,500)	(8,875)
Deferred tax	(1,500)	(1,000)	(625)
Profit after tax	9,500	9,500	9,500

Notes:

1) The timing differences will start to reverse from year 6 onwards and the higher tax liabilities will be reduced in the accounts by transfers from deferred tax account.

2) The balance on deferred tax account at end of year 3 is £3,125 (credit). This can be reconciled as follows:

Written down value in accounts	£13,000
Less written down value for tax	6,750
Difference	6,250 at 50% = £3,125.

Footnote on history: ED 11 (May 73) full provision, urged deferral method. SSAP 11 (Aug 75) full provision, permitting deferral or liability (postponed to Dec 76, later withdrawn). ED 19 (May 77) partial provision, liability method. SSAP 15 (Oct 78) partial provision, permitting deferral or liability. Revised (May 1985) liability only.

Notes

SSAP 16   Current cost accounting

Issued March 1980 – mandatory status
suspended June 1985, now withdrawn

As a result of the withdrawal of SSAP 16 there is now an almost universal lack of interest in it as far as accounting practice is concerned.

SSAP 16 is still important in the study of accounting for inflation and also in relation to accounting theory. The ASC state that it 'remains an authoritative reference on accounting under the current cost convention'. The following notes therefore are confined to those aspects of SSAP 16 which I consider have aided the search for alternative accounting conventions.

Appendix 3 (page 173) contains a more detailed commentary on the inflation accounting debate, including points from the ASC Handbook which was issued following the withdrawal of SSAP 16.

Background

Outline of post-war developments

Statement by ICAEW in 1952 recognized the limitations of Historic Cost Accounting (HCA) but found alternative conventions proposed at that time to be unacceptable. The statement requested members to advise management of the need to retain sufficient earnings to cover higher replacement costs. During 1970/73 the ASC worked on a standard for Current Purchasing Power (CPP) accounting. In January 1974 the government set up the Sandilands Committee on Inflation Accounting and in May 1974 the ASC issue a provisional standard (SSAP 7) on CPP accounting. In 1975 Sandilands rejects CPP and proposes CCA as complete replacement of HCA. Sandiland proposals accepted by ASC (with some minor amendments) and ED18 issued in 1976. In 1977 members of ICAEW passed a resolution rejecting compulsory CCA as required by ED18. The ASC issued an interim recommendation (generally called 'Hyde guidelines') which required a Current Cost Profit Statement to be included with certain published accounts. In March 1980 SSAP 16 adopted on a three year trial basis.

Developing the standard

Points considered
In most systems of accounting profit is determined after making charges against revenue to provide for maintenance of capital and since the definition of capital varies so the concept of profit will vary. In HCA the charges against revenue include the original cost of any assets (stock and fixed assets) consumed in earning that revenue. Where input prices are rising the profit under HCA contains no charge against revenue to recognize the increased cost of replacing what has been consumed and thus does not provide for the maintenance of capital in terms of the real operating assets.

Underlying idea
The CCA system uses a concept of capital which is represented by the net operating assets expressed at current cost. A change in the input prices of assets used up will affect the funds required to maintain these operating assets and CCA is designed to reflect this in both the determination of profit and in the balance sheet.

Outline of the standard

Publish CCA in addition to HCA either by presenting HCA as the main accounts with supplementary CCA or vice versa. CCA prepared by making adjustments to the HCA figures to allow for the additional funds required to maintain the operating capability of the business. Adjusted by transferring amounts to a Current Cost Reserve (CCR) in respect of fixed assets, stocks and monetary working capital. Offset these adjustments with a 'gearing adjustment' where the business is partly financed by borrowings. Assets in the balance sheet revalued (through CCR) and stated at 'their value to the business' based on current price levels.

Definitions and concepts used in the standard

Value to the business
Net current replacement cost or, where recognized as lower, the recoverable amount. Recoverable amount is defined as the greater of net realizable value and the amount recoverable from further use.

Depreciation adjustment
Difference between the HCA depreciation charge and the proportion of fixed assets, at 'value to the business', consumed during the current period. Note that the wording used in the SSAP meant that any 'backlog depreciation' was not charged to CCA profit and loss account but was dealt with through the CCR. Backlog depreciation is depreciation not provided in previous years as a result of an uplift in value during the current year. Consequently under SSAP 16 the total replacement cost was not charged against profit.

Cost of sales adjustment (COSA)
Difference between the HCA cost of sales and the 'value to the business' of stock consumed during current period. Guidance notes suggested a number of ways of determining this including use of indices and the LIFO method of determining cost of sales.

Monetary working capital adjustment (MWCA)
An extension to COSA recognizing that additional finance would be needed to replace stocks if input prices rose between the date of sale and the date cash was received from debtors. The use of trade credit for purchases has a compensating effect and therefore the MWCA was based (roughly) on trade debtors less trade creditors.

Gearing adjustment
An adjustment to relieve CCA profit of a proportion of the three CCA operating adjustments based on the proportion of capital financed by net borrowing. The total CCA operating adjustments would normally be a debit to CCA profit when prices were rising and therefore the gearing adjustment would have been a credit to profit and a debit to CCR.

Current cost operating profit
Historic cost profit (before interest) less CCA adjustments for depreciation, cost of sales and monetary working capital.

Current cost profit attributable to shareholders
Current cost operating profit plus the gearing adjustment, net of interest paid, and after extraordinary items.

Net operating assets
Comprise: fixed assets (including trade investments), stock and monetary working capital. To be carried in the CCA balance sheet at value to the business. Monetary working capital is already at such value in the HCA.

The operating capability of the business
The amount of goods and services which the business is able to supply with its existing resources during the relevant period. The resources are represented in accounting terms by the 'net operating assets' at current cost. The capital maintenance concept in SSAP 16 was often referred to as maintaining the operating capability of the business.

Cross-references

CA 1985
Includes both historic cost and alternative accounting rules (AAR). The combined effect is to permit accounts to be prepared in one of three ways, i.e. HCA only, CCA only, or HCA modified by the revaluation of certain assets. The Act stipulates bases to be used for revaluations under the AAR and in some cases these must be at 'current cost' although tangible fixed assets may be stated at current cost or the

market value on the date they were last valued. Current cost is not defined in the Act and if a company decides to use current cost as the basis (not likely to be popular) presumably the principles established by SSAP 16 would have to be used.

Standards
(i) All other standards apply to CCA. (ii) The source and application of funds statement is required to be compatible with whatever basis is used as the main accounts. (iii) IAS 15 requires the effect of changing prices on certain items to be presented. The items concerned are depreciation, cost of sales, monetary items and borrowing. Any method of inflation accounting may be used, e.g. CPP or CCA. If CCA is used the current cost of physical assets must be disclosed. The information can be presented on a supplementary basis.

Illustration

The following illustrates the purpose and mechanics of COSA:
Details: The opening balance sheet of a business consists of 100 items of stock which cost £10 each (£1,000 in total). During the period the opening stock was all sold for £1,400 and expenses of £200 were incurred. The balance of £1,200 was used up in replacing the stock with 100 similar items which had increased in cost to £12 each.

Accounts under HCA

Profit and loss for period				Balance sheets	
Sales		£1,400	Opening		Closing
Less: Cost of sales:					
Opening stock	1,000		1,000	Stock at cost	1,200
Purchases	1,200				
	2,200				
Closing stock	1,200	1,000	1,000	Capital	1,000
GROSS PROFIT		400		Add Profit	200
Expenses		200			
NET PROFIT		200	1,000		1,200

Note that the business has not increased the volume of its net operating assets over the period and yet a profit of £200 has been reported. Any distribution (or taxation) of the £200 would have resulted in a reduction of the operating capability because the remaining funds would not have been enough to purchase another 10 items. HCA does not therefore make sufficient charge against revenue to provide for the maintenance of the operating assets.

Adjustments under SSAP 16 using the 'averaging method' to determine COSA
Details: If it is assumed that the index for the stock items at the beginning of the period was 100 then it would have risen to 120 by the

end of the period when the closing stock was purchased. The average index for the period is therefore 110. The averaging method normally assumed that the total purchases in HCA would reflect the average price per unit for the period and whilst this may not be the case in this example the assumption is treated as holding good in order to demonstrate the basic simplicity (and fairness) of the method.

Cost of sales adjustment

Opening stock at average price (110/100)	1,100
Purchases (assumed at average)	1,200
	2,300
Closing stock at average price (110/120)	1,100
	1,200
Cost of sales in HCA	1,000
	200

In the current cost accounts the COSA of £200 would be debited to profit and credited to CCR leaving profit at nil so that the final balance sheet would be as follows:

Stock at cost	1,200	Capital	1,000
		CCR	200
		Profit	nil
	1,200		1,200

A summary of the latest debate on inflation accounting appears in Appendix 3 on page 173.

Notes

SSAP 17   Accounting for post balance sheet events

Issued August 1980

Background

Business
No particular influence except that the cut-off date was sometimes used to 'window dress' accounts by processing a transaction (e.g. a sale to related undertaking) before the year end and reversing it afterwards. Refer to Pergamon Press affair for an example.

Accounting
Practice of searching post balance sheet period for transactions which would help in assessing the position at the accounting date was already a well established procedure. Recommendations on the subject had already been made by the individual accountancy bodies. Sometimes the requirements of an existing SSAP involved consideration of post balance sheet events, e.g. dividends receivable from an associate company under SSAP 1.

Developing the standard

Points considered
Post balance sheet period should end on the date accounts approved by directors. Balance sheets attempt to give accounting measurements of conditions which exist at the accounting date. Events which occur during the post balance sheet period may provide further evidence on which to make a judgement of these conditions. Some events relate to conditions which arose subsequent to the accounting date and although no adjustment to the accounts is needed the event itself may require disclosure so as to assist users in making proper decisions and evaluations.

Basic approach adopted
Events occurring during the post balance sheet period to be identified as being either adjusting events and non-adjusting events.

Definitions

Post balance sheet events
Those, both favourable and unfavourable, which occur between balance sheet date and date when financial statements are approved by the directors.

Adjusting events
Post balance sheet events which provide additional evidence of conditions existing at balance sheet date. Includes events where statute or convention requires them to be reflected in the financial statements.

Non-adjusting events
Post balance sheet events which relate to conditions that arose subsequent to the the balance sheet date. (SSAP 17: 'did not exist at'.)

The standard

Financial statements
Should be prepared on basis of conditions existing at the balance sheet date.

Material post balance sheet event requires adjustment to the figures
Either where (a) it is an 'adjusting event', or (b) it indicates that the going concern concept is not appropriate.

Material post balance sheet event requires disclosure
If it is either: (a) a non-adjusting event, or (b) it is the reversal (or maturity) of a transaction entered into before the year end where its purpose was primarily to alter the appearance of the balance sheet (i.e. a window dressing transaction).

Presentation and disclosure

Adjusting events
Do not require disclosure, they merely provide evidence in support of measurements used in the financial statements.

Non-adjusting events and 'window dressing' reversals
If sufficiently material disclose: nature of event and an estimate of its financial effect before tax. The tax implications should also be explained if material.

Date
Disclose date on which financial statements were approved by directors.

Cross-references

CA 1985

Two references: (1) 'Accounting Principles' in Part II Sch. 4 requires all liabilities and losses for the year to be taken into account 'including those which only become apparent between the balance sheet date and the date on which it is signed on behalf of the board' (adjusting events), and (2) post balance sheet events of the non-adjusting type must be disclosed in the directors report.

Standards

(i) Change of exchange rates is given as an example (see below) of a non-adjusting event but presumably there may be situations where it can be classed as an adjusting event e.g when estimating the rate on maturity of a long-term monetary item as required by SSAP 20 – see illustration 4. (ii) The provisions in IAS 10 dealing with post balance sheet events accord with SSAP 17.

Extract of some examples given in the appendix

Adjusting events	*Non-adjusting events*
Fixed asset: sale proceeds or purchase price determined for any transactions entered into before year end	Purchase or sale of fixed assets and investments after year end
Valuations: which provide evidence of a permanent diminution in value of property or long-term investments	Decline in value of fixed assets shown to have occurred after year end
Stocks and work in progress: any sale proceeds which give evidence of net realizable value. Evidence relating to long-term contracts	Losses of stocks or fixed assets through catastrophe after the end of the year
Debtors: renegotiations or insolvency	**Mergers** or other extensions of business activities
Tax rates: information on rate changes	**Exchange rate** changes – but see illustration 4
Dividends receivable: declaration of proposed dividend by an associated company	**Government action** such as the nationalization of material part of the business

Note

In exceptional circumstances an event which would otherwise be classified as non-adjusting may require changes to the financial statements in addition to disclosure, e.g. where its impact is of such magnitude as to negate application of the going concern concept.

Illustrations

1) **During the post balance sheet period a fire occurred in one of the company's factories and the uninsured loss is estimated at £500,000.**

Comment: On the face of it this appears to be a non-adjusting event since the condition (loss of factory) occurred subsequent to the accounting date. It would only be classed as an adjusting event if it is of such impact as to impair the company's ability to carry on as a going concern. If this is not the case and the loss is considered material it should be disclosed. The company will then have to decide where to make the disclosure.

The SSAP requires disclosure in the 'notes to financial statements' and the CA 1985 requires disclosure in the 'directors' report'. If the company decides to only disclose the event in one of these two places there should be a cross reference from one to the other.

2) **During the post balance sheet period the company receives notification that a debtor, thought to be good at the accounting date, has gone into liquidation. The amount outstanding is £300,000.**

Comment: This would be classed as an adjusting event if the anticipated loss is considered material since the condition (an amount receivable) existed at the balance sheet date. The notification may give some indication of how much is likely to be paid to creditors and this could be used to estimate the likely loss and extent of the adjustment (increase in provision for bad debts). No additional disclosure is necessary unless the expense is considered exceptional under SSAP 6.

3) **The accounts included the sale during the final week of the year of £600,000 to a company which is not in the group but is controlled by the managing director of the holding company. It was discovered that these same goods had been purchased back from the managing director's company by a wholly owned subsidiary of the reporting group in the week following the accounting date.**

Comment: On the face of it this appears to be a blatant window dressing transaction. But care would be needed to establish the circumstances since the requirement to disclose the event (the purchase back by the group) centres on whether the intention in the first place was to alter the appearance of the balance sheet. Intentions are difficult matters on which to conclude and there may be a rational explanation. Where the problem is being considered by an auditor it might be necessary to obtain legal advice.

4) **A UK company raised a long-term loan during the current period from a foreign country called Pololand. The loan was 1,400,000 Polos and the sterling proceeds were £100,000. At the balance sheet date the exchange rate was £1 = 15 Polos but during the post balance sheet period there was a major currency realignment in**

Pololand and the exchange rate of the Polo to the £ has been devalued to £1 = 20 Polos.

Comment: SSAP 20 requires long-term monetary items which are denominated in foreign currency to be translated at each accounting date and any gains or losses to be treated as ordinary profit or loss for the year. The guidance notes state that it will not be easy to predict what the exchange rate is likely to be on maturity and a best estimate should be made 'in the light of the information available'. The year-end rate is only suggested as providing the best estimate in most cases. In the above example it seems that more information is available which can be used in making the estimate. Since it will now only cost £70,000 to repay the loan there seems to be good reason for restating the loan and reporting a profit of £30,000.

Notes

SSAP 18   Accounting for contingencies

Issued August 1980

Background

Accounting and law
CA 1967 required disclosure by way of note of contingent liabilities not provided for, and details of charges on assets securing loans of other persons. Prudence concept requires contingent gains to be excluded and for a contingent loss to be accrued if the outcome is expected to be a loss.

Developing the standard

Points considered
Treatment of contingencies should be determined by their expected outcome. Where it is probable that the outcome will confirm a loss it should be accrued. Prudence excludes the accrual of contingent gains. In those cases where there is reasonable certainty that the gain will be realized it is not a contingency and an accrual is appropriate. Where the uncertainties result in non-accrual a contingent loss should be disclosed by way of note but contingent gains should only be disclosed if realization is probable.

Definitions

Contingency
A condition existing at balance sheet date where outcome will be confirmed only by occurrence, or non-occurrence, of one or more uncertain future events. A **contingent gain or loss** is one dependant upon the contingency.

The standard

Material contingent loss
Accrue if it is probable that the future event will confirm the loss and the amount can be estimated with reasonable accuracy. If not accrued under this requirement, e.g. because of uncertainties, disclose by way of a note unless possibility of loss is remote.

Material contingent gain
Not accrued. Only disclose by way of note if probable that gain will be realized.

Presentation and disclosure

Contingencies disclosed by way of note
Nature of contingency, uncertainties affecting outcome, prudent estimate of financial effect made at date accounts approved by directors, or statement that such estimate not practicable. In the case of losses disclose any amount accrued and any element considered remote.

Cross references

CA 1985
The CA 1967 provisions are carried over into CA 1985.

Standards
SSAP 2, accruals and prudence. IAS 10 accords closely to SSAP 18.

Interesting points

Semantics and principles
The accruals and prudence concepts are applied to contingencies through a minefield of adjectives. Losses are accrued if **probable** and estimates of loss **reasonably accurate**, otherwise noted unless **remote**. Gains are not contingent and should be accrued if receipt is **reasonably certain**, but only noted where realization is **probable**. Presumably 'probable' means: more evidence for than against.

Examples

No examples are given in the standard but students may find the following list helpful.
  Guarantees given for loans and overdrafts granted to third parties. There is a loss contingent upon the lender enforcing the guarantor to repay under terms of the guarantee. If assets of the reporting company

are used as security for the loans of other persons particulars of the charge must also be given to comply with CA 1985.

Legal and insurance claims against or by the company. The loss (or gain) is contingent upon the outcome of the case. Even when a judgement has been made the case may be subject to appeal in a higher court.

Investments in partly paid shares. There is a liability contingent upon the directors of the investee company making a call on the shares.

Deferred tax. Legal advice taken by the ASC suggests that any deferred tax not provided would be a contingent liability in some cases but see SSAP 15 which has its own disclosure requirements in this respect.

Illustrations

1) **A holding company has guaranteed a bank loan of £500,000 granted to an associated company. The associated company is trading profitably and is relatively solvent.**

Comment: There is no question of a contingent loss to be accrued since there seems to be no question of the bank calling in the loan. Even if it were there may be sufficient assets in the associate to satisfy the bank's demands. A loss to the guarantor is contingent upon the bank calling in the loan and the associated company being unable to pay up. The contingent loss should be disclosed as a note except where the possibility of loss is remote.

2) **A company has been defending a court case in respect of a claim for damages relating to an alleged act of negligence. During the post balance sheet period judgement was given against the company by the High Court and an award of £500,000 damages was made. The company is taking the case to the Court of Appeal although no date for the hearing had been set by the time the accounts were approved.**

Comment: In the absence of any persuasive arguments otherwise it would seem that this loss should be accrued.

3) **During the accounting year the company started a court action against a competitor for alleged breach of copyright. During the post balance sheet period the court found in favour of the company and awarded it £50,000 damages. Correspondence with the solicitors indicates that the defendant company has no intention of appealing and will be settling the damages awarded.**

Comment: This is not a contingent gain but an actual gain and should be accrued. If there was some question over settlement, e.g. a possible appeal by the defendant it is a contingent gain which should only be noted if its realization is probable.

Notes

Notes

SSAP 19 Accounting for investment properties

Issued November 1981

Background

Business
Property investment companies objected to SSAP 12 which required all assets with finite life to be depreciated. They argued (contrary to SSAP 12) that any loss arising from a reduction in economic life of buildings would be offset by increases in value of the land and yet SSAP 12 would require them to take revaluation surpluses to reserve and depreciation of buildings to profit.

Accounting
Temporary exemption to SSAP 12 for investment properties.

Developing the standard

Points considered
Investment properties are not held for consumption in the course of business but as investments, the disposal of which would have no material affect on the trading or manufacturing operations. In this case their current value and changes in that value, rather than depreciation, are more appropriate to the appreciation of the financial position.

Basic approach and method
Investment properties exempted from SSAP 12 and a form of current value accounting prescribed.

Definitions

Investment properties
Interest in land and/or buildings where construction and development completed and held as investment for rental income negotiated at arm's length.

Exceptions to definition

Property owned by company for own purposes or let to another member of the group.

The standard

SSAP 12 exemption

Investment properties, other than leaseholds with unexpired term of 20 years or less, should not be subject to periodic depreciation charge.

Carrying value

Open market value. Changes in value not taken to profit and loss but shown as movements on investment revaluation reserve. Excess deficits on revaluation reserve must be charged to profit and loss.

Presentation and disclosure

Valuation details

Names of valuers or particulars of their qualification. Basis of valuation. Whether valued by employee or officer.

Balances

Carrying value of investment properties and investment revaluation reserve should be displayed prominently.

Various Exceptions

Not applicable to charities. The revaluation reserve does not apply to pension funds and long-term business of insurance companies where changes in value are dealt with in a relevant fund account. Charging excess deficits to profit may not be appropriate for investment trust companies (see SSAP 6) or property unit trust companies.

Cross-references

CA 1985

Investment properties are not defined nor otherwise dealt with. The provisions of SSAP 19 are a departure from the depreciation rules but this is covered by the Sec 228 'true and fair' override. Under Sec 228 the effect of not depreciating would have to be disclosed and by implication the depreciation would have to be calculated, thus negating the purpose of SSAP 19.

    This conflict was discussed between the ASC and DTI and according to Bulletin number 20 of 'True and Fair' it seems that the requirements of Sec 228 are met if the accounting policy note includes words similar to the following:.

. . . Depreciation or amortisation is only one of many factors reflected in the annual valuation and the amount which might otherwise have been shown cannot be separately identified or quantified.

Standards
SSAP 6 and 12 as referred to in these notes. There is no equivalent IAS.

Interesting points

Principles
(i) If current value accounting is prescribed for property investments there may be a case for applying it to other fixed investments. Since changes in current value are not passed through the profit and loss account, the SSAP is seen as a pragmatic solution to a particular case. The merit of its theoretical base is open to question. (ii) The short lease exception recognizes that it would be inconsistent to amortize the reduction in value against reserves whilst rentals are taken to profit.

Problems
The SSAP does not require a professional valuation except that the explanatory notes suggest a 'major enterprise (e.g. a listed company)' which has substantial investment properties should have them valued:

1) annually by a person with a recognized professional qualification and who has had the relevant experience; and
2) at least every five years by an external valuer.

Notes

Notes

Notes

SSAP 20   Foreign currency translation

Issued April 1983

Background

Business
Growing international trade in the form of transactions with foreign entities and extending operations by setting up a business unit in an overseas country, usually as a subsidiary but sometimes as a branch.

Accounting
An abundance of techniques described in textbooks but practice favoured a method which became known as the 'closing rate' method. Lack of agreement over how to deal with translation differences.

Developing the standard

This SSAP contains over six pages of notes which explain and justify practices prescribed in the standard. The following extract is therefore a little longer than usual but in order to avoid too much repetition (a predicament of SSAP 20 itself) some explanations are omitted here and dealt with in 'the standard'.

POINTS AND PRINCIPLES CONSIDERED

Accounting problems arise from foreign currency operations in two situations:

1) **Transactions** which are denominated in a foreign currency and have not been settled by the balance sheet date. These could relate to any business dealings with a foreign person such as a supplier, bank, branch, subsidiary etc.
2) **Translation** of financial statements for an overseas subsidiary or branch which are produced in their local currency and need to be consolidated with the accounts of the UK concern.

Translation is required in both cases and any changes in exchange rates will cause gains or losses to arise which must be accounted for. Methods prescribed should produce results generally compatible with the effects of rate changes on the cash flow and on the equity of the reporting company.

Translation differences
Gains or losses caused by currency movements which impact on cash flows should be treated as part of profit for the year. If not reflected in cash flows they should be recorded as a movement on reserves.

Foreign branch or subsidiary
Methods of translation and impact of currency movements on cash flows can be determined from the financial and operational relationship which exists with the overseas entity, namely:

Separate and quasi-independent foreign entity
There is an investment in the net worth of a foreign entity which will remain until it is liquidated or the investment is sold. The 'closing rate' method gives the fairest translation of the foreign entity's net worth. Currency movements will cause gains or losses to arise on translation but they have no real impact on current cash flows.

Foreign entity dependent on, and interlinked with, UK company
The foreign entity is seen as an extension of the UK company. The financial statements of the foreign entity can be translated as if every transaction had been entered into by the UK company. The 'temporal method' of translation is therefore more appropriate and currency movements will be reflected in cash flows.

Definitions

Foreign enterprise
Foreign subsidiary, associated company or branch.

Translation
Process whereby financial data denominated in one currency are expressed in terms of another. Relates to expression of individual transactions and expression of financial statements.

Closing rate
Exchange rate for spot transactions on balance sheet date based on the mean of buying and selling rates at close of business.

Temporal method
Not defined in the SSAP but explained in notes as being on the same basis as for the 'individual company stage' (see below) which is to record transactions at rate when incurred and re-translate any monetary items not cleared by the year end to the closing rate.

Net investment
Effective equity stake comprising investing company's share of foreign enterprise's net assets.

Monetary items
Money and amounts to be received or paid in money. Categorized as short-term (falling due within one year) or long-term.

The standard

Approach
Standard procedures considered in two stages, namely:

1) preparation of financial statements of an **individual company**; and
2) preparation of **consolidated** financial statements.

Students should note that the first relates to any company which undertakes transactions payable or receivable in foreign currency and is not unique to companies with a foreign branch or subsidiary.

1) INDIVIDUAL COMPANY

Transactions
Recorded at rate when incurred. Thereafter non-monetary assets are carried at their translated amount. Monetary items unsettled at accounting date should then be translated to the closing rate. Gains or losses arising on settled transactions and on unsettled short-term monetary items are (or soon will be) reflected in cash flows and should be recorded as profit. Contracted rates are to be used in the translation process where appropriate.

Long-term monetary items
Such as loans payable. Not possible to predict likely rate on maturity and best estimate in light of information available should be made, generally year end rate. Gains or losses on translation recognized as part of profit under accruals concept, cash basis would not be consistent with that concept. Prudence may make it necessary to restrict recognition of gains where conversion of currency is doubtful.

Transactions with subsidiaries
Same as for transactions with third parties.

Cover or offset
Applies where foreign equity investments financed by foreign borrowings, usually as 'hedge' against exchange risks. Translate investment to closing rate each year. Resulting gains or losses taken to reserves and gains or losses on translation of borrowings first offset against reserve movement. Gains or losses on borrowings may only be offset to the extent of differences arising on translation of investment. Borrowings used in offset process should not exceed the cash flows expected to be generated by the investment.

2) CONSOLIDATION

Closing rate (net investment) method
Should normally be used.

Exchange differences
Arising from translation of opening net investment to closing rate must be recorded as a movement on reserves.

Profit and loss account
Where financial statements are dealt with under the closing rate method the profit and loss account may be translated at closing or average rate. The average rate should be weighted where appropriate and the difference between profit and loss at average rate and at closing rate should be recorded as a movement on reserves.

Temporal method
Should be used where trade of the foreign enterprise is more dependent on the economic environment of the investing company's currency than on its own. Since exchange gains or losses are reflected in cash flows they are recognised as part of the profit for the year.

Examples where temporal may be appropriate
Explanatory notes suggest three, i.e. where the foreign enterprise:
1) acts as selling agency of goods supplied by investing company and remits proceeds of sale back the company;
2) produces raw materials (or parts) which are shipped to investing company for inclusion in its own products;
3) is located overseas for tax, exchange control, or similar reasons enabling it to raise finance for group members.

Cover or offset
Conditions same as for individual company except that it only applies where relationship of foreign enterprise is such as to justify closing rate method for translation of net assets. If applied in investing company's own accounts for investment which is neither subsidiary nor associate the same procedure may be used in the consolidated accounts.

Disclosure

Methods of translation and treatment of exchange differences
Gains or losses on foreign borrowings, identifying any amount offset and any amount dealt with in profit and loss account. Net movement on reserves arising from exchange differences.

Cross-references

CA 1985
Does not deal with translation. Gains or losses recognized as part of profit under the SSAP fall to be treated as realized 'in accordance with principles generally accepted'. The SSAP states that unrealised gains or losses on long-term monetary items are covered by the 'true and fair' override. Gains or losses included in profit are classified as 'other operating income or expense' or 'other interest and similar items' according to their origin.

Standards

IAS 21 is similar in many respects to SSAP 20 but does suggest and allow for gains or losses on translation of long-term monetary items to be deferred and amortized over the remaining life of the monetary item.

Interesting points

Changes in exchange rates during the post balance sheet period are given as an example of a non-adjusting event in SSAP 17 but the translation of a long-term monetary item at the balance sheet date under SSAP 20 requires a best estimate of the rate on maturity to be made. Closing rate is suggested as a possible basis but presumably a post balance sheet rate could be used in some cases.

The standard does not require a separate reserve for translation gains and losses when the closing rate method, or cover principle, is being used although some companies are doing so. The implication is that these gains and losses are unrealized but the only requirement is that they are shown as adjustments to reserves and not as profits and losses for the year. This has resulted in some companies dealing with them as movements on the balance of 'retained earnings' and examples of where this has happened are included in Appendix 1.

Illustrations

1) TRANSACTIONS

A UK company purchased a fixed asset on credit from France costing FFr90,000 when £1 = FFr9. The creditor was outstanding at the accounting date of 31 March when the rate was £1 = FFr10. Payment was made one month later when £1 = FFr11.25

Comment: The fixed asset will be recorded at (90,000 ÷ 9) £10,000. This is a non-monetary asset and will not be subject to any further translation. Depreciation is based on £10,000. The creditor is initially recorded at £10,000 but must be restated at the balance sheet date to (90,000 ÷ 10) £9,000. This results in a gain of £1,000 which is included in ordinary profit. The amount paid to clear the creditor in the following period is (90,000 ÷ 11.25) £8,000 and a further of gain of £1,000 arises which is also treated as ordinary profit.

2) COVER OR OFFSET – INDIVIDUAL COMPANY

A UK company has a 10% equity investment in a French company which cost FFr90,000 when the exchange rate was £1 = FFr10. At the same time, as a hedge against exchange losses, the UK company borrowed FFr45,000 to partly finance the investment. By the end of the year the £ had weakened and the rate was £1 = FFr9.

Comment: The investment is initially recorded at £9,000 and the borrowing at £4,500. At the end of the year the borrowing is translated to (45,000 ÷ 9) £5,000 and the £500 loss would normally (without the cover principle) be debited to profit but it can be offset against a gain of £1,000 on the investment if it is translated to (90,000 ÷ 9) £10,000 as allowed by SSAP 20. The reserve movement will then a net gain of £500. The cover or offset procedure is permissive (not mandatory) but if adopted must be applied consistently.

3)   CONSOLIDATION USING CLOSING RATE METHOD – WITH COVER FOR LOSS ON LOAN

The holding company acquired a 100% interest in a Pololand subsidiary at the beginning of the year when the exchange rate was £1 = 5 Polos. At the same time it borrowed P400 to help finance the investment. The closing rate was £1 = 4 Polos.

Balance sheet of holding company

	Original	*Trans-lated*		*Original*	*Trans-lated*
Investment in subsidiary:			Share capital	500	500
Cost (P800 at P5 = £1)	160		Retained profits	400	400
At closing rate (800 ÷ 4)		200	Translation reserve		
			(40 − 20)		20
Sundry net assets	820	820	Loan P400 (at P5) & (at P4)	80	100
	980	1,020		980	1,020

Balance sheet of Subsidiary

	Polos	*Trans-lated*		*Polos*	*Trans-lated*
Sundry net assets	1,000	250	Share capital and reserves:		
			At acquisition	700	140
			For year	300	75
			Gain on translation		35
	1,000	250		1,000	250

Consolidated balance sheet

Goodwill (160 − 140)		20	Share capital	500
Sundry net assets		1,070	Retained profits (400 + 75)	475
(820 + 250)			Translation reserve	
			(35 − 20)	15
			Loan	100
		1,090		1,090

Notes: In the consolidation it is the gain on translation of the net investment (net assets) which provides the cover for the loss on the loan. The gain of £35 results from restating the opening net assets from £140 (700 ÷ 5) to the closing rate (700 ÷ 4) i.e. £175.

Notes

SSAP 21   Accounting for leases and hire purchase contracts

Issued August 1984

Background

Business
Figures produced by the Equipment Leasing Association (ELA) show that there was a tenfold increase in annual expenditure on leased assets between 1973 and 1983 (from £288m to £2,894m). The largest part of the business was with the finance subsidiaries of clearing banks who dominate membership of ELA. The growth in popularity of leasing as a form of medium-term finance can be related to economic and taxation factors prevalent during this period.

Accounting
Methods of income recognition prescribed by SSAP 21 are based on what is commonly known as the investment period principle. This had already evolved and had been established as the basis for best practice by members of ELA. Lessee accounting was less uniform. Common practice for finance leases was to treat rentals as a revenue expense, leaving the asset used and its financing as 'off balance sheet' items.

Developing the standard

POINTS CONSIDERED

Lessors
Fall into three broad categories, namely:

1) financial institutions providing finance to enable a single customer to obtain use of asset for most of its useful life;
2) companies renting out assets for varying periods, often to more than one customer;
3) manufacturers and dealers who use leases as a means of marketing their own products.

Lessor and lessee
As they are party to same transaction the same definitions can be used

and practices for each should be complementary (mirrored) although balances will differ due to tax and cash flow consequences.

Forms of lease
Can appropriately be classed as 'finance leases' or 'operating leases' depending on terms of contract between lessor and lessee, as follows.

Finance lease: Lessee agrees to make payments to lessor which will cover cost of the asset together with a return on finance provided. Most of the risks and rewards of ownership, other than legal title, pass to lessee.

Operating lease: Lessee pays a rent for hire of asset for a period usually less than its useful economic life and lessor retains most of the risks and rewards of ownership.

BASIC APPROACH AND METHOD

Finance lease
Lessee to capitalize the rights acquired (describe as leased asset) and at the same time recognize an obligation to make future payments. Rentals paid allocated between reduction of obligation and finance charge. Hire purchase (HP) contracts normally treated in a similar way. Lessor to record net investment in the lease as a debtor. Rentals received allocated between gross earnings and reduction of debtor. Gross earnings to be recognized at a constant periodic rate of return on the net cash investment in the period.

Operating lease
Lessor to treat asset as fixed asset and depreciate in normal way. Rentals treated as expense by lessee and income by lessor.

Definitions

The SSAP contains eighteen definitions and the following is a summary of those considered to be more important. Some definitions are linked to others which makes it difficult to form a mental image of what is being defined. The more awkward of these are clarified by illustrations at the end of the notes.

Finance lease
One that transfers substantially all the risks and rewards of ownership to lessee. Such transfer presumed if, at inception, the present value of minimum lease payments (including any initial payment) is substantially all (normally 90% or more) of the fair value of the asset. Present value calculation to be based on the interest rate implicit in lease. Presumption may be rebutted.

Operating lease
One other than finance lease.

Minimum lease payments

Payments due over remaining term of lease. For lessee they are the amounts he expects to pay, which include any residual amount he guarantees. For lessor they are amounts he expects to receive and retain, which include any residual amount guaranteed by lessee or an independent third party.

Gross investment in the lease

Minimum lease payments plus any unguaranteed residual value accruing to lessor.

Net investment in the lease

Gross investment in the lease less gross earnings allocated to future periods. (Note: at inception this will normally be the cost of the asset less any grants received.)

Net cash investment in the lease

Funds invested by lessor which take account of all related cash flows i.e cost of asset; government grants; rentals received; taxation; interest paid on any borrowings to fund the lease, or received on surplus funds generated by the lease; profit taken out of the lease; residual value at end of lease term. (Note: this is purely a memorandum calculation.)

Interest rate implicit in lease

A discount rate which, if applied to minimum lease payments and unguaranteed residual value, will give a present value equal to fair value of leased asset. If not determinable by the lessee it can be estimated by reference to rates applicable to similar leases.

Finance charge

An amount borne by lessee being the difference between minimum lease payments (MLPs) and amount at which asset recorded by lessee at inception of lease. (Note: MLPs include residual amounts which lessee guarantees.)

Gross earnings

Difference between lessor's gross investment in the lease and the cost (net of grants received) of the leased asset.

Initial direct costs

Those incurred by lessor relating to the negotiation of leasing agreements such as commissions, legal fees, credit investigations.

The standard

Hire purchase

Those of financing nature (usual) treat as for finance lease.

LESSEE ACCOUNTING – FINANCE LEASES

Asset and obligation on inception

Record both at the present value of minimum lease payments found by discounting them at implicit interest rate. In practice the fair value of the asset (price at which it would be exchanged on an arm's length transaction) will be sufficiently close and may be used.

Rentals paid
Apportion between finance charge and reduction of obligation. The finance charge should be allocated to accounting periods so as to produce a constant periodic rate of charge on the amount outstanding for each period.

Depreciate
Over shorter of lease term or useful life. Assets acquired under HP agreements should be depreciated over their useful lives.

Operating leases
Rentals charged as expense, usually on a straight line basis.

LESSOR ACCOUNTING – FINANCE LEASES

Balance sheet
Record as debtor for the net investment in the lease.

Gross earnings
Allocate to accounting periods so as to give a constant periodic rate of return on the **net cash investment** in the lease in each period. Net cash investment (memorandum) differs from balance sheet debtor (net investment) because it recognizes cash flows other than rentals. With HP net investment will usually approximate to net cash investment because the lessor's tax cash flows are not affected by capital allowances on the asset. (*Note*: capital allowances on assets subject to finance leases are usually granted to lessor, with HP they are granted to lessee.) Reasonable approximations may be made.

Initial direct costs
Apportion over period of lease. (*Note*: with finance leases this is usually done by deducting initial costs from gross earnings on inception so that only the balance of gross earnings is spread over the lease period.)

Tax free grants for leased assets
Spread over period of lease and treat as non-taxable income or gross up and include with profit before tax.

Lessor accounting – operating leases
Record as a fixed asset and depreciate over useful life. Rentals treated as income, usually straight line basis.

Manufacturer/dealer
Selling profit under finance lease restricted to excess of fair value of asset over manufactured or purchase cost (net of any grants).

Sale and leaseback
Occurs when own property is sold (e.g. to a finance company) and then leased back by former owner. The lease should be accounted for

in the same way as any other lease. Treatment of profits or losses on disposal depend on type of lease, namely:

if finance lease the seller/lessee should amortise over the shorter of the lease term or useful life of asset.

if operating lease recognise immediately except where sale proceeds differ from fair value. Excess of sale price over fair value should be deferred and amortised; if sale price is below fair value the profit or loss should be recognised immediately – except that if apparent loss is compensated for by rentals below market price then to this extent it should be amortised.

Disclosure

Assets held under finance leases
May be combined with owned assets (cost and depreciation) providing net book value of leased assets disclosed, otherwise show as separate category. Depreciation expense for year separately disclosed.

Net obligations
By lessee under finance leases analysed between (a) amounts due within next year, (b) amounts due in second to fifth years, (c) aggregate amounts due thereafter. Equivalent information for HP contracts.

Operating lease rentals
Amount charged as expense in year analysed between plant hire and other rentals. Note of commitments analysed between those due in next year, the second to fifth, and thereafter. Commitments for land and buildings separated from others.

Lessor
Cost of assets acquired for letting as finance leases.

Cross-references

CA 1985
Formats do not deal with leased assets. Lessee's obligations (and lessor's debtors) will have to be separated between amounts due within one year and those due after more than one year.

Standards
(i) Deferred tax (SSAP 15) needs to be considered on finance lease rentals. In the case of a lessee the pattern of expenditure in accounts (finance charge and depreciation) is likely to be different to the rentals paid which will be allowed for tax. Lessors also have timing differences caused by capital allowances. (ii) No conflict with IAS 17 which tends to be more general and is less onerous on disclosure.

Interesting points

Semantics
(i) There was a conceptual change between exposure draft and SSAP which removed the idea of 'substance over form' for assets capitalized under a finance leases. ED 29 intended the leased asset itself to be capitalized whereas the SSAP states that it is the right to use the asset which is capitalized. Since the lessee is only capitalizing something he is legally entitled to there is no application of substance over form. (ii) The word 'obligation' is used since the credit balance is not a debt in the legal sense of the word but an obligation to make future payments under a bailment to hire.

Principles
(i) The SSAP argues that the asset capitalized under a finance lease is the lessee's right to the use of the asset. In principle this would make it an intangible asset but the standard allows it to be combined with tangible owned assets. In this respect the standard does recognize the substance of the asset rather than its technical form. (ii) In principle the carrying value of this right should be measured on the basis of the present value of the minimum lease payments (present value based on a discount rate equal to the implicit interest rate). Since by definition this value will be at least 90% of the fair value in most finance leases, the fair value of the asset can be used as an approximation. (iii) The basic concept applied is accruals (or matching) e.g. in the case of the lessor more income is recognized at the start of the lease where finance costs and bad debt risks are higher.

Practice
(i) If a contract is to be treated as a lease for tax (allowing lessee to charge rentals as an expense) the lessor is not allowed to sell the residual to the lessee. Consequently most finance leases are structured so that at the end of the primary period either (a) the asset is sold to a third party and between 95% to 97% of sale proceeds are given back to lessee as a rent rebate, or (b) the lessee continues to lease the asset at a nominal (sometimes called 'peppercorn') rental. (ii) In most cases there will be no need to carry out complicated present value calculations to determine whether a lease is a finance lease. If the lessor's interest in the unguaranteed residue is 10% or less (as it would be if 95% to 97% of the sale proceeds are rebated to lessee) it will fall within the definition because this percentage would be even smaller in present value terms. Note that one of the risks of ownership is a loss in the value of the asset and the 90% test is simply a way of recognizing cases where the lessor bears very little (10% or less) of this risk.

Illustrations

1) DEFINITIONS

The following details are not meant to illustrate a typical lease structure. They are contrived simply to show the relationships between certain definitions in SSAP 21: Lease term = 3 years; Rentals = 3 annual of £10,000; Residual value at end of lease term = £5,000 (none of which will be rebated to lessee); Residual amount guaranteed by an independent insurance company = £4,000; Cost of asset to lessor = £28,000

Lease as viewed by lessor:

Minimum lease payments:	
– Rentals (3 x £10,000)	30,000
– Residual amount guaranteed by insurance company	4,000
	34,000
Unguaranteed residual value: (5,000 − 4,000)	1,000
Gross investment in lease:	35,000
Gross earnings to be allocated to future periods:	(7,000)
Net investment in the lease on inception (i.e. cost)	28,000

Note that the lessee's minimum lease payments are £30,000 since the £4,000 guaranteed by the insurance company is not payable by the lessee or a party related to him. The presence of third party guarantees can sometimes mean that a lease will be classified as an operating lease by a lessee and a finance lease by a lessor. This is illustrated by the following:

Manufacturer's normal selling price (fair value)	4,000
Purchased by finance company and leased	
out for 3 annual rentals of £1,000	3,000
Estimated residual value	2,000
Manufacturer guarantees to buy back from	
finance company at end of lease for	1,800

Comment: There is no need in this case to perform present value calculations in order to classify the lease. As far as the lessee is concerned his minimum lease payments (3,000) are less than 90% of the fair value even before they are discounted. On this basis the lessee would classify it as an OPERATING lease. As far as the lessor is concerned the unguaranteed residual value (£200) is already less than 10% of fair value before discounting and so he would classify it as a FINANCE lease.

2) PRESENT VALUE OF MINIMUM LEASE PAYMENTS

This concept is the basis for the capital value of a finance lease in the lessee's books. On inception the fair value of the asset usually gives a close approximation to it (see 'interesting points'). Apart from exams there will not be many situations where a lessee would not know the fair value. It could arise if there was only one supplier and the product was only available for leasing through a finance company.

Of the various ways in which a student may be asked to work out present values the most likely (until computers are part of the exam process) is to give discount factors from present value tables. The following example shows how they would be used to calculate the present value of minimum lease payments of three annual rentals of £1,000 payable in advance if the implicit interest rate is 10%

Year	Payment	Discount factor	Present value
0	1,000	1.00000	£1,000
1	1,000	0.90909	909
2	1,000	0.82645	826
	3,000		2,735

The lessee should capitalize the asset at £2,735. The difference between this and the total payments (3,000 – 2,735) is £265 which represents the finance charge. It should be allocated to accounting periods at a constant periodic rate on the balance outstanding in the period. This is quite simple and is illustrated next.

3) LESSEE ACCOUNTING

Using the figures in example 2 the lessee will initially record an asset of £2,735 and an obligation of £2,735. The asset will be depreciated in accordance with the standard. If the useful life is not less than 3 years and no residual value accrues to the lessee the £2,735 will be depreciated over 3 years using an acceptable method.

The annual rentals are split between finance charge and reduction of obligation. The periodic finance charge can be found by working in reverse through the present value calculations in example 2 so that the charge for the first year is (1,000 – 826) £174, for the second year it is (1,000 – 909) £91 and for the third year (1,000 – 1,000) nil. Note that payments are in advance and so there is nothing outstanding during the third year. The periodic finance charge can be proved (and rental allocation illustrated) as follows:

Year	Obligation at start of period	Rental paid	Obligation during period	Finance charge at CPR of 10%	Reduction of obligation	Obligation at end of period
1	2,735	1,000	1,735	174	826	1,909
2	1,909	1,000	909	91	909	1,000
3	1,000	1,000	–	–	1,000	–
		3,000		265	2,735	

The 'sum of digits' method (see example 5) may be used and would give similar results.

4) SELLING PROFIT RESTRICTION – MANUFACTURER/DEALER

This problem is concerned with what is commonly known as 'sales aid leasing', i.e. where a business offers concessionary leasing rates in order to market its own products. Normally a business entering into a finance lease with a customer should recognize the full selling profit (normal selling price less cost) immediately as if it had been sold. The gross earnings under the lease will be the difference between the normal selling price and the amounts which the lessor expects to receive and retain. These are allocated over the lease in the normal way.

If concessionary leasing rates are offered the selling profit must be restricted so that a full commercial rate is imputed to the gross earnings element of the lease. This involves the calculation of a notional selling price. For example assume the lease in examples 2 and 3 was written by a dealer and that the asset cost him £2,000 which he would normally sell for cash at £2,735. If commercial rates for the lease are rentals of £1,050 per annum he should treat it as being sold for $1,000/1,050 \times 2,735 = 2,605$. The reduced selling profit of £605 is recognised straight away and the gross earnings of $(3,000 - 2,605)$ £395 allocated over the lease period. If you have access to a computer spreadsheet program you will find that if the rentals had been 1,050 per annum the implicit interest rate is 16% and this rate is used for the periodic allocation of gross earnings by the dealer/lessor.

5) HIRE PURCHASE – LESSOR

The following simplified examples show how repayments would be allocated between income and capital using two different methods. *Details*: cost of asset to finance company = £1,000; HP payments = 4 of £275 each payable quarterly in advance.

The gross income is £100, i.e. rentals (4 × 275) £1,100 less cost £1,000.

(a) Sum of digits method: The formula for sum of digits is $n(n + 1) \div 2$, with n being the number of periods to which an amount has to be allocated.

Period	Income Fraction	Amount	Capital	Total
1	3/6	50	225	275
2	2/6	33	242	275
3	1/6	17	258	275
4	0	0	275	275
Totals	6/6	100	1,000	1,100

Notes: No income is allocated to the last period as payments are in advance. The number of periods is 3 and so the sum of the digits is 6 (i.e. 3 × 4 ÷ 2).

(b) Actuarial (before tax) method:

Net investment start of period	Cash flows out	in	Net investment during period	Gross earnings at CPR of 6.75%	Net investment end of period
0	1,000	275	725	49	774
774		275	499	34	533
533		275	258	17	275
275		275	0	0	0
		1,100		100	

Notes: The allocation of gross earnings is similar to the sum of digits method in (a). The constant periodic rate of 6.75% has to be found by programmed calculator, actuarial tables, computer, trial and error (together with interpolation methods), or it is given in exams.

6) FINANCE LEASE – CONSTANT PERIODIC RATE OF RETURN ON NET CASH INVESTMENT (NCI)

This principle requires the lessor to make an estimate of the average amount of cash invested in the lease, for the various periods to which the gross earnings are allocated. The task of forecasting all cash flows associated with a lease is quite involved. The timing of tax payments has to be considered as well as the pattern of funding costs or funding income (when surplus funds are created and could be invested) as a result of writing the lease.

The standard requires the 'profit taken out of the lease' to be added back to the receipts and payments. The justification for this is that the profit generated by the lease is used to meet indirect costs and pay dividends and therefore is not available to reduce the level of cash invested in the lease.

The following simplified example uses the lease in example 5 but assumes the four periods are four years. This makes the implicit interest rate unrealistic as far as annual rates are concerned but does enable a comparison to be be made with 5(b). For simplicity it also assumes that the lessor has no interest payments – as would be the case where the entire funding is through equity. In order to see the effect of tax payments over the four year period it is further assumed that the asset is sold at the end of the lease for its tax written down value and all proceeds are rebated to the lessee. Writing down allowances are 25%, the tax rate is 35% and is payable during the year following that in which the profit was earned.

The taxable profit created by the lease is £100 and this arises over the four years in the form of rentals received (less rebate) less the capital allowances claimed on the cost of the asset. In the circumstances assumed, tax paid would be: Year 1 nil, Year 2 £9, Year 3 £32, and in Year 4 there would be tax recoverable of £6 – making total tax £35 over the four years. In order to make it easier to trace the effect of such insignificant figures the calculations below bring in the whole £35 as a payment in Year 3.

Two methods are commonly used to allocate gross earnings at a CPR on the NCI. They are: the Investment Period Method (IPM) and the Actuarial after tax method. In both cases the first stage is to calculate the periodic NCI. In doing this the after tax profit (£65) taken out of the lease must be at a CPR on the NCI. The rate has to be found by the various processes mentioned previously and in this example it refines to 4.42%. The following calculates NCI in the first table and shows allocation of gross earnings under IPM in the second:

| | | | | FIRST STAGE | | | SECOND STAGE | |
| | | | *Determine periodic net cash investment:* | | | | *Allocation of gross earnings Investment period method:* | |
NCI at start	Cash flows out	Cash flows in	NCI during period	Profit taken out 4.42%	NCI at end	NCI fraction	Gross earnings
0	1,000	275	725	32	757	757/1535	49
757		275	482	21	503	503/1535	33
503	35	275	263	12	275	275/1535	18
275		275	0	0	0	0/1535	0
Totals	1,035	1,100		65	1,535		100

The 'actuarial method after tax' takes the periodic profit (after tax) figures from the NCI table and by using this as the bottom line of the profit and loss account it works back to the top in order to find gross earnings. In the above example there are no interest payments to consider and so the gross earnings can be found by simply grossing up the profit after tax, e.g. Year 1: 32 ÷ 0.65 = £49. In this example the allocation will be the same as under IPM but the two methods can produce different results when interest payments and receipts are included in the calculation of NCI.

Where interest is built in to the NCI table it would be calculated at the specified rate on each period's NCI and included in a separate column before the profit take out column. The tax payments would change because of the interest and the profit to take out will be based on gross earnings less interest and tax.

Notes: Net cash investment calculations are purely memoranda and the profit on all leasing finds its way into the profit and loss account through conventional nominal ledger totals. None of the figures in the NCI table are used in the books and the calculations are only made to find the capital portion of rentals received during the period. The capital portion is deducted from the rentals received and credited to net investment (the debtor) leaving the gross earnings element of the rentals as a credit in the profit and loss account.

Notes

Notes

SSAP 22   Accounting for goodwill

Issued December 1984, revised July 1989

Background

Business

Earlier practices tended to treat purchased goodwill as a permanent asset. Some companies had been writing off goodwill, even before being required to do so by CA 1981 (now 1985).

More recently, companies have become concerned by the effect of writing off large amounts of goodwill and have attempted to replace this was an asset called 'Brands'. The matter is subject to much debate, at present the ASC appears to consider that brands are merely another name for goodwill.

Accounting

Actively debated by academics but little uniformity in practice other than the exclusion of non-purchased goodwill. CA 1981 influenced change.

The revision of SSAP 22, in July 1989, included a number of additional disclosure requirements. These seem to be aimed at certain creative accounting practices which had become opportune when dealing with business combinations – e.g. creating excessive provisions in the accounts of the acquired entity and then releasing them during the post-acquisition period. Motives for this practice could have been to give a favourable impression of the new management. The disclosures required are intended to help users distinguish between trading performance of the combined entity and other factors such as the release of provisions set up when the combination occurred.

Law

EEC fourth directive required goodwill to be written off over a maximum period of five years but allowed member states to derogate from this providing goodwill written off over a period not exceeding its useful economic life. On implementation through CA 1981 power to derogate was exercised.

Developing the standard

POINTS CONSIDERED

Main characteristic
Incapable of being realized separately from the business as a whole. *Also*: its value has no predictable relationship to costs incurred; intangible factors contributing to goodwill (e.g. specialist skills) cannot be valued; value is highly subjective and fluctuates according to circumstances.

Purchased goodwill
Arises when a business combination is accounted for as an acquisition. It includes goodwill arising on consolidation, on acquisition of an interest in associate company, and on purchase of an unincorporated business.

Non-purchased goodwill
Exists where the business as a going concern is worth more than the total fair value of its separable net assets. Not recognized in accepted practices since it is not evidenced by a purchase transaction.

Both types compared
Although purchased goodwill is established as a fact at a particular point in time by a market transaction, there is no difference in character to non-purchased. Both involve the subjective valuation of a business.

Immediate write-off
Of purchased goodwill does not imply a loss in value and should be seen as an accounting policy consistent with that of not including non-purchased goodwill.

An alternative view
Of purchased goodwill is that it is a real asset which has been paid for, it exists and should be treated like other capital assets.

Basic approach and method
Immediate write-off preferred method. Should be made against reserves. Should not be treated as a charge against profit since the write-off is not related to results for the year. The write off is a matter of accounting policy consistent with that of excluding non-purchased goodwill from financial statements.

Amortization
Against profit over estimated useful economic life to be allowed in recognition of the alternative view of goodwill.

Different acquisitions
May be considered separately and different policies adopted in each case so as to allow companies to meet their circumstances such as carrying insufficient reserves for an immediate write-off.

Definitions

Goodwill
Difference between value of business as a whole and the aggregate of the fair values of its separable net assets (see also SSAPs 1, 14 and 23).

Separable net assets
Those which can be identified and sold (or discharged) separately without the need to dispose of the business as a whole. Includes identifiable intangibles such as patents.

Purchased goodwill
Established from the purchase of a business accounted for as an acquisition. Goodwill arising on consolidation is one example.

Non-purchased goodwill
Any goodwill other than purchased.

Fair value
Amount which could be exchanged in an arm's length transaction.

The standard

Non-purchased goodwill
Should not be included in any financial statements.

Purchased goodwill
Should not include any value for separate intangibles and should not be carried as a permanent item. Should normally be eliminated from the accounts by immediate write off against reserves.

Negative goodwill
Must be credited directly to reserves.

Amortization method
Permitted. The charge should be against profit or loss on ordinary activities for the year and based on useful economic life estimated at time of acquisition. Amortization period may be shortened but not increased. The amount not written off should never be revalued except to recognize any permanent diminution in value to be charged to profit and loss account.

Different acquisitions
Considered separately and either policy adopted.

Disclosure

Accounting policies. Goodwill acquired during year. If amortization policy is adopted, show movements during year and state amortization period selected.

Additional disclosure required by the revised SSAP (see Background) can be summarized as follows:

1) For each acquisition, show fair value of consideration given, amount of goodwill arising, and how goodwill has been dealt with in the accounts.
2) Provide a table showing:
   book values of acquired company at the date of acquisition;
   fair values of each major category of asset and liability.
   Differences between these values should be explained and analysed under:
   revaluations;
   provisions for future losses;
   other provisions;
   alignment of accounting policies with those of the acquiring group;
   any other major item.
3) As regards disposal of an acquired entity (or segment), the following must be disclosed:
   profit or loss on disposal;
   amount of purchased goodwill attributable to the disposal and how this was treated in determining the profit or loss;
   if cases where proceeds of sale are treated as a reduction in costs of acquisition, disclose the proceeds and how dealt with in the accounts.

Cross references

CA 1985
Most requirements which originated in CA 1981 (now CA 1985) are followed in the SSAP. Formats prescribe disclosure. Goodwill not written off immediately to be amortized over a period chosen by directors (not exceeding useful economic life) who must explain the reasons for choosing that period.

Standards
The international standard on goodwill is part of IAS 22 called 'Accounting for business combinations', see reference in SSAP 23. The goodwill provisions are similar in many respects to SSAP 22 but there is a requirement that negative goodwill should either be: treated as deferred income and amortized to profit on a systematic basis, or allocated over the depreciable non-monetary assets acquired in proportion to their fair values.

Interesting points

Principles
An appendix deals with legal implications of the immediate write-off method on the definition of realized profits as follows:

(a) The problem is not relevant to group accounts since distributions are made by individual companies.

(b) Immediate write-off is an accounting policy and not the recognition of a loss but since SSAP 22 is based on a concept that goodwill has limited life its elimination must eventually constitute a realized loss. If written off against unrealized reserves, transfer to realized on a systematic basis so as to maintain parity with the amortization method. In cases of doubt seek legal advice.

(c) Legal restrictions on the revaluation reserve may prevent it from being used to write off goodwill.

(d) Negative goodwill may be released to realized reserves in line with depreciation of other assets in the acquisition.

The suggestion made in (d) seems to be in line with the IAS 22 requirement mentioned under 'cross-references' above.

The revised SSAP contains additional appendices. One of these (Appendix 1) discusses factors relating to the determination of useful economic life, but comes to the conclusion that it is not possible to specify any general rules. There is also an example of a fair value table (Appendix 3) as required by the amended disclosure requirements.

Fair value

The ASC are developing an accounting standard on fair value in the context of acquisition accounting. The following points have been extracted from their discussion paper:

(a) fair value of shares given as consideration, at price prevailing immediately prior to bid announcement;

(b) fair value of assets acquired, viewed by acquirer according to intentions – i.e. usually replacement price if intention is to keep, and realizable value if intention is to sell;

(c) raw materials, at replacement cost;

(d) work in progress and finished goods, at selling price less profit and the sum of costs for completing and selling;

(e) provisions for future trading losses of a continuing business should not be made;

(f) determine fair value at date of acquisition, but allow a hindsight period (e.g. up to the date of publication of the first accounts affected by the fair value exercise);

(g) provision made for any deferred tax implications.

Illustrations

1. ACQUISITION OF A BUSINESS

Company A acquires the unincorporated business of 'Pronto Printers' as a going concern. The relative figures of Pronto Printers are as follows:

	Book value	Fair value
Patents	12,000	12,000
Tangible net assets	80,000	100,000
	92,000	112,000

Company A considers that the business can generate maintainable profits of £30,000 per annum and is looking for a return on capital of 20%. It therefore valued the business of Pronto Printers at £150,000. This amount was accepted by the owners of Pronto Printers and paid by Company A.

Comment: The payment of £150,000 in Company A's books will be allocated as follows:

Patents	12,000
Net tangible assets	100,000
Goodwill	38,000
	150,000

If Pronto Printers had been an incorporated business and Company A had acquired a 100% interest by paying £150,000 to the shareholders for their shares the payment would be recorded as an investment. The above figures would then be incorporated into the consolidated balance sheet and the £38,000 would be described as goodwill arising on consolidation.

2. WRITING OFF GOODWILL

Assume that Company A in Example 1 had acquired the unincorporated business and had the following reserves: Revaluation reserve £138,000, Other undistributable reserves £50,000, distributable reserves £28,000. *Comment*: It could decide to amortize the goodwill against profit over its estimated useful economic life. If it decided to adopt an immediate write-off policy it would have to consider the following points:

(a) For legal reasons it probably cannot use the revaluation reserve.
(b) It does not have sufficient distributable reserves against which it can be written off.
(c) It can write it off against undistributable reserves. If it decided to do this it should make an annual adjustment to transfer an amount from undistributable reserves to distributable reserves. The systematic amount could be based on the estimated economic life of the goodwill acquired.

3. NEW DISCLOSURE REQUIREMENTS

The following fair value table and notes are reproduced from Appendix 3 of the revised standard.

Fair value table
Acquisition – XYZ LTD *Date* – 19.2.89

Consideration – 100,000 £1 ordinary shares were issued to acquire the following assets. The fair value of the consideration, using the mid-market price on 19.2.89 of £3.06, was £306,000, giving rise to goodwill of £100,000.

	Book value £000	Revaluation £000	Provisions for trading losses £000	Other provisions £000	Accounting policy alignment £000	Other major items £000	Fair value to the group £000
Fixed assets							
Intangible	—	—	—	—	—	80 [f]	80
Tangible	160	20 [a]	—	—	—	—	180
Investments	20	5 [b]	—	—	—	—	25
Current assets							
Stock	40	—	(4) [c]	(5) [d]	(2) [e]	—	29
Debtors	35	—	—	—	—	—	35
Investments	10	—	—	—	—	—	10
Cash at bank	12	—	—	—	—	—	12
Total assets	277	25	(4)	(5)	(2)	80	371
Liabilities							
Provisions:							
Pensions	30	—	—	—	—	—	30
Taxation	45	—	—	—	—	10 [g]	55
Other	10	—	8 [c]	—	—	—	18
Creditors:							
Debenture	2	—	—	—	—	—	2
Bank loans	15	—	—	—	—	—	15
Trade creditors	30	—	—	—	—	—	30
Other creditors	10	—	—	—	—	—	10
Accruals	5	—	—	—	—	—	5
Total liabilities	147	—	8	—	—	10	165
Net assets	130	25	(12)	(5)	(2)	70	206

Adjustments	Explanations
(i) Revaluations	
Note a	Increases in value of freehold properties since last revaluation in 1981.
Note b	Increase in value of shares of USM investment since purchase in 1983.
(ii) Provisions for Trading losses	
Note c	Losses expected to be incurred prior to closing down small tools division.
(iii) Other provisions	
Note d	Write-down following reassessment of realisable value of stock which is more than one year old.

(iv)   **Accounting
            policy alignments**

            Note e   Change of stock valuation from weighted
                                    average cost to FIFO which is used by the
                                    group.

(v)   **Other major
            Items**

            Note f   Recognition of intangibles – relating to
                                    publishing titles and brands acquired.

            Note g   Adjustment to deferred tax arising from
                                    the incorporation of fair values.

Notes

Notes

SSAP 23 Accounting for acquisitions and mergers

Issued April 1985

Background

Business

A popular way of combining two businesses is for one of the companies to acquire the shares in the other by issuing its own shares as consideration. Technically there has been an acquisition in such a way as to allow each company to carry on as separate entities. In substance, however, there is a merger whereby the two companies are jointly owned by a united body of shareholders in the holding company. When acquisition accounting is used the pre-acquisition profits of one company in the merger (the subsidiary) cannot be made available for distribution to this united body of shareholders.

Accounting

Merger accounting (also called pooling) was developed as a means of overcoming this problem. It had been practised in USA for some time and was evolving in UK. In 1971 the ASC issued ED 3 on merger accounting but it never became an SSAP due to legal conflicts which remained unresolved until CA 1981.

Law

Merger accounting only works if the investment in the subsidiary is carried in the holding company's books at nominal value of the shares issued. There were conflicting views over whether the Companies Act required a share premium account to be written up in such cases. The matter was eventually decided by the Court in a tax case called Shearer v Bercain Ltd in 1980. The ruling was that the investment must be recorded at fair value of the shares issued and any excess of fair value over nominal value should be credited to share premium account. This made merger accounting impossible until CA 1981 provided a relief which exempted the issuing company from the requirement to account for the share premium in certain types of merger. The relief is called 'merger relief'.

Developing the standard

POINTS CONSIDERED

Group accounts
Two methods have been developed, namely:

Acquisition accounting Results of acquired company only consolidated from date of acquisition. Assets of acquired company stated at cost to acquiring group. The effect is similar to the acquisition an unincorporated business.

Merger accounting Financial statements aggregated and presented as if the two companies had always been together.

Criteria for appropriate method
Merger accounting when combination results mainly from a share for share exchange leaving two groups of shareholders in a position to continue as before but on a combined basis. Acquisition method when consideration paid to the former owners results in substantial resources leaving the group.

BASIC APPROACH AND METHOD

Merger accounting acceptable
Providing that the consideration given for equity is such that no more than 10% of its fair value is in a form other than equity in the issuing company. This ensures that acquisition accounting will have to be used when substantial resources leave the group in a form such as cash or loan stock.

Definitions

Business combination
One or more companies become subsidiaries of another.

Offer
Any offer made by 'the offeror' for shares in another ('offeree'). Offers in a composite transaction are treated as a single offer.

Effective date of acquisition
Earlier of (a) when consideration passes; or (b) when offer becomes, or is declared, unconditional.

Equity share capital
The issued share capital excluding any part which only carries the right to participate in a distributions up to a specified amount.

The standard

Merger accounting
May be used if certain conditions are met, namely:

1) the business combination results from an **offer to all equity holders** and to all holders of voting shares not already held by the offeror, and
2) as a result of the offer the offeror **secures at least 90% of the equity** and of shares which carry at least 90% of the votes of the offeree, and
3) immediately before the offer the offeror **did not hold 20% or more of the equity**, or 20% or more of the votes, of the offeree, and
4) **not less than 90% of the fair value of consideration given** for equity shares, including that for shares already held, is in the form of equity shares.

Conditions not met
Account for as an acquisition.

Acquisition accounting
Fair value of consideration given should be allocated according to provisions of SSAP 14 (group accounts) and SSAP 22 (goodwill). The results of the acquired company only brought in from date of acquisition.

Merger accounting
Net assets of subsidiary consolidated using book values. Consolidated profit and loss (including comparatives) not adjusted to exclude profits earned prior to acquisition.

Consolidation adjustments in merger accounting
Arise when value of investment in holding company's books (being at nominal value of shares issued) differs from the nominal value of shares acquired. Account for as follows:

carrying value of investment is less than nominal value of shares acquired, treat difference as a reserve on consolidation, and where

carrying value of investment is greater, treat as a reduction of reserves. The word goodwill should not be used as this involves recording fair values of subsidiary's separable assets whereas merger accounting uses book values.

Applicable to other forms of business combination
Although the standard refers to an acquiring company issuing shares as consideration for shares in another company it should be read as applying to any arrangement which achieves similar results, e.g. formation of a new holding company which acquires a controlling interest in two or more existing companies. Merger accounting may be adopted in this case if the appropriate conditions are met.

Disclosure – merger accounting

Notes to group accounts
Should include the fair value of consideration given by issuing company.

Consolidated profit
An analysis between pre- and post-merger for the year. Pre-merger profit (including comparatives) analysed between holding company and subsidiary. Extraordinary items analysed into pre- and post-merger events, and a statement as to which party in the merger the items relate.

Cross-references

CA 1985
Secs 131–134 deal with merger relief. They apply if a company obtains at least 90% of the equity holding in another company through an issue of its own equity shares. Merger relief exempts the issuing company from the requirement to account for any share premium on issue and thereby allows the investment to be carried at nominal value of the shares issued.

These provisions only relate to accounting in the holding company's books and do not directly legislate for merger accounting. The conditions attached to the relief are less stringent than those in SSAP 23 for merger accounting. There is no requirement for 90% of the consideration to be in the form of equity shares and no corresponding provision regarding the 20% former holding.

Standards
The institutional regulatory framework has become a little untidy with provisions for group accounts now spread over SSAPs 1, 14, 22, and 23. This is likely to be rationalized after the EC 7th directive is adopted.

IAS 22 deals with accounting for business combinations and includes provisions on mergers similar in some respects to those in SSAP 23. Being an international standard it is not as definitive as the UK domestic standard on the situations in which merger accounting may be used.

Interesting points

Principles
The standard only deals with group accounts. Accounting in the holding company's books is covered by an appendix as follows:

The carrying value of the investment
Will normally depend on the method to be adopted in the group accounts, namely:

in acquisition accounting at cost which will be at the fair value of any consideration given.

in merger accounting at nominal value of shares issued plus the fair value of any consideration given in a form other than equity shares.
  Where a holding company carries the investment at fair value in circumstances where merger relief is available the excess of fair value over nominal value of shares issued should be credited to a separate merger reserve. Where the relief is not available the excess must be credited to share premium account.
  Where merger accounting applies it seems that any dividends received from the subsidiary out of profits earned prior to acquisition can be treated as profit, unlike acquisition accounting where they are treated as capital.
  The reasoning behind the 20% prior holding restriction is thought to be because the investment would have been dealt with as an associated company. This would not be compatible with merger accounting since fair values are used.

Developments
Following the issue of this SSAP, some combinations have been accounted for as a merger in circumstances which complied with the letter of the SSAP but not its spirit (e.g. vendor placings). The ASC intends to tighten the rules which permit merger accounting. Refer also to SSAP 22 for a recent revision of that standard, and for notes on the fair value discussion paper.

Illustrations

1) MERGER CONDITIONS

H already owned 50 equity shares in S which it acquired some time ago for cash at a cost of £60. It now acquires the remaining 450 equity shares by issuing 450 of its own £1 equity shares, with a market value of £900, to the shareholders in S.
  Consideration summarized (at nominal and fair value) as follows:

	Nominal	Fair
Prior investment (50 shares) paid in cash	£60	60
Shares issued on merger (450 shares)	450	900
Total	510	960

Conditions satisfied because (1) prior investment was less than 20% and (2) although equity shares issued on the merger form less than 90% of nominal value of total consideration (£510) they do form more than 90% of its fair value of £960.

2) CONSOLIDATION

Four different situations are illustrated based on balance sheets of two companies which, before any entries on the share issue, stood as follows:

Company A:		Company B:	
Net tangible assets	400,000	Net tangible assets	300,000
Share capital (£1 equity shares)	300,000	Share capital (£1 equity shares)	100,000
Reserves	100,000	Reserves	200,000
	400,000		300,000

Market value of A's shares is £3.60 each. Fair value of B's net assets is £350,000.

Group balance sheets (ignoring SSAP 22) for each situation under both methods are:

Situation 1

All shareholders in B accept 1 share in A for 1 of their shares in B:

	Acquisition method			*Pooling method*
Net tangible assets				
(400,000 + 350,000)	750,000	(400,000 + 300,000)		700,000
Goodwill (360,000 – 350,000)	10,000			—
	760,000			700,000
Share capital (A's)	400,000	(A's)		400,000
Share premium				
(A's = 100,000 × £2.60)	260,000	(A's = nil)		—
Reserves (A's only)	100,000	(A's + B's)		300,000
	760,000			700,000

Situation 2

Only 90% of B's shareholders accept the offer, remaining 10% reject it:

	Acquisition method			*Pooling method*
Net tangible assets				
(400,000 + 350,000)	750,000	(400,000 + 300,000)		700,000
Goodwill (324,000 – 315,000)	9,000			—
	759,000			700,000
Share capital (A's)	390,000	(A's)		390,000
Share premium				
(A's = 90,000 × £2.60)	234,000	(A's = nil)		—
Reserves (A's only)	100,000	(A + B – MI)		280,000
Minority interests				
(10% × 350,000)	35,000	(10% × 300,000)		30,000
	759,000			700,000

Situation 3

All of B's shareholders accept 11 shares in A for 10 of theirs in B:

Net tangible assets			
(400,000 + 350,000)	750,000	(400,000 + 300,000)	700,000
Goodwill (396,000 – 350,000)	46,000		—
	796,000		700,000
Share capital (A's)	410,000	(A's)	410,000
Share premium			
(A's = 110,000 × £2.60)	286,000	(A's = nil)	—
Reserves (A's only)	100,000	(A's + B's)	300,000
Adjustment to reserves	—	(110,000 – 100,000)	(10,000)
	796,000		700,000

Situation 4

All of B's shareholders accept 9 shares in A for 10 of theirs in B:

Net tangible assets			
(400,000 + 350,000)	750,000	(400,000 + 300,000)	700,000
Negative goodwill			
(324,000 – 350,000)	(26,000)		—
	724,000		700,000
Share capital (A's)	390,000	(A's)	390,000
Share premium			
(A's = 90,000 × £2.60)	234,000	(A's = nil)	—
Reserves (A's only)	100,000	(A's + B's)	300,000
Consolidation reserve	—	(90,000 – 100,000)	10,000
	724,000		700,000

Footnote: Students are warned to be careful over how they use the words merger and acquisition. They are used mainly as labels for the two methods of accounting. In a merger there is still a holding company and subsidiary relationship for which consolidated accounts are required.

Notes

SSAP 24   Accounting for pension costs

Issued May 1988

Background

Pension costs can form a significant part of total payroll costs. In some cases, they give rise to special problems of estimation and allocation between accounting periods.

Developing the standard

Points considered

Most pension schemes are funded – i.e. benefits are paid out of funds accumulated in a separate scheme, internal or external to the company. Such pension schemes are basically of two types:

1) defined contribution;
2) defined benefit.

Defined contribution schemes: employer makes contributions to a pension scheme. Retirement benefits paid to the employee depend on contributions and investment earnings of the scheme. Cost to the employer can be measured with certainty.

Defined benefit schemes: benefits depend on pay of the employee, either on average pay or (more typically) final pay. Cost is subject to uncertainty since it is not possible to determine in advance if contributions (together with investment earnings) will be sufficient to cover the benefits promised. Periodic actuarial valuations will be required, which may reveal deficiencies or surpluses.

Basic approach and method

Accounting objective: employee considers pension as deferred remuneration, employer views it as part of the cost in obtaining the employee's services. Employer should recognise cost on a systematic and rational basis over the period during which benefits are received from the employee's service.

With defined contributions schemes, systematic annual cost will be the same as the actual contributions paid in the year.

With defined benefit schemes, periodic actuarial valuations may result in employer having to provide further funds, or show that past contributions have been excessive.

The effect of these 'experience surpluses or deficits' should not be treated as a prior year adjustment. Variations from regular pension costs should be allocated over the expected average remaining service lives of employees in the scheme. This may involve making a provision where annual contributions are reduced as a result of a surplus, or a prepayment where annual contributions are increased to make good a deficit.

Note: many of the explanatory notes in SSAP 24 are concerned with ensuring that actuarial valuation methods satisfy the accounting objective. In view of the interprofessional co-operation that exists between accountants and actuaries, such points are not covered in this guide.

Definitions

There are 17 definitions in the standard and several deal with terminology used in actuarial valuations. These specialized terms are not included in the following notes.

Pension scheme
An arrangement to provide pension (and/or other benefits) for members on leaving service or retiring and, after death, for their dependants.

Accrued benefits
Benefit for service up to given point of time, whether rights are vested or not. May be on current earnings or protected final earnings.

Funded scheme
Where future liabilities for benefits are provided for by the accumulation of assets held external to the company's business.

Defined benefit scheme
Where the rules specify the benefits to be paid, and the scheme is financed accordingly.

Defined contribution scheme
Where benefits are determined by the value of contributions.

Ex gratia **pension**
One which the employer has no legal commitment to provide.

Pensionable payroll/earnings
Earnings on which benefits and/or contributions are calculated. Adjustments may be made to exclude certain elements such as overtime, or reductions that recognize state benefits.

Average remaining service life
A weighted average of the expected future service of current members,

up to normal retirement dates or expected dates of earlier withdrawal or death.

Past service
Is used in the standard to denote service before a given date, not to service before entry into the scheme.

Regular cost
The consistent ongoing cost recognized under the actuarial method used.

Experience surplus or deficiency
That part of the surplus or deficiency of the actuarial value which arises because events have not coincided with the assumptions made for the last valuation.

The standard

Applicability
Statement deals with pensions, but principles may apply to other retirement benefits. Not applicable to state contributions or redundancy payments.

Pension cost
Recognize expected cost on a systematic and rational basis over the period during which benefits are received from the employee.

Defined contribution schemes
Charge against profits should be the contributions paid in the period.

Defined benefit schemes
Costs should be calculated using actuarial valuations. The method of providing for expected pension costs should be such that regular pension cost is a substantially level percentage of current and future payroll.

Variations from regular cost should normally be allocated over the expected remaining service lives of current employees in the scheme. Average remaining service lives may be used. The following three exceptions apply:

1) Where a major event or transaction has occurred, outside the normal scope of actuarial assumptions, prudence may require a material deficit to be recognized over a shorter period than remaining service lives. An example given in the guidance notes relating to this is where there has been a major mismanagement of a pension scheme's assets.

2) A significant change in contributions in order to eliminate a surplus or deficiency resulting from a reduction in number of members. Any reduction in contributions should be recognized as it occurs, although amounts receivable should not be anticipated – e.g. the full effect of a contribution holiday should be spread over its duration.

3) Where a refund to the employer is made and this is subject to tax, the surplus or deficiency may be accounted for in the period of the refund.

Ex gratia pensions, and *ex gratia* pension increases
To be recognised as a cost when granted.

Disclosure

There are too many requirements for students to remember them in detail. As would be expected, full details of the scheme, provisions or prepayments made, results of the most recent actuarial valuation, commitments to make additional payments, accounting policy, are all included.

Cross references

CA 1985
Disclosure of: pension commitments, including separate disclosure of those to past directors; total pension costs for the year; disclosure of pensions paid to past directors, except those funded through a pension scheme; contributions paid into a funded scheme for a director must be treated as part of that director's emoluments for disclosure purposes.

Standards
Redundancies may have to be considered as extraordinary under SSAP 6. Since this requires items derived from a single event to be aggregated, it may not be appropriate to defer recognition of any related pension cost or benefit. Pension costs charged in the accounts may differ from the amounts paid (and allowed for tax) and there could be a deferred tax implication to be dealt with under SSAP 15. The accounts of the pension scheme itself are covered by SORP 1. SSAP 24 is compatible with IAS 19.

Illustrations

1) An actuarial valuation carried out at the end of year 1 shows that the pension scheme fund has a surplus of £6 million. The pension scheme actuary has recommended that the surplus should be eliminated by making reduced contributions for the next 3 years of £3 million and then to return to the normal contribution of £5 million each year. The average remaining service life of members is 10 years.

Discussion

In order to spread pension costs evenly over the next ten years, the charge in the profit and loss account each year needs to be one-tenth of £44m (i.e. (3 × £3m) + (7 × £5m)). This amounts to £4.4m each year.

But the amount actually being paid each year for the next 3 years is only £3m and therefore the company should credit a provision (and debit pension costs) with £1.4m each year for the next three years. After 3 years, the provision will amount to (3 × £1.4m) £4.2m.

For the next 7 years, the company will pay £5m each year, and in order to reduce pension charges in the profit and loss account to £4.4m it will debit the provision (credit pension costs) with £0.6m each year. The provision of £4.2m will therefore be eliminated (7 × 0.6) by the end of the 10th year.

2) A company's annual contribution to the pension scheme is £5m. An actuarial valuation at the end of the current year shows a deficit of £6m. The actuary has recommended that the deficit be eliminated by making a total contribution £8m in the next year, and an increased contribution of £6m for the next 3 years, reverting to the normal payment of £5m each year thereafter. Remaining service lives of employees averages to 10 years.

Discussion

In order to spread pension costs evenly over the next 10 years, the charge in the profit and loss account each year needs to be one-tenth of £56m (i.e. (1 × £8m) + (3 × £6m) + (6 × £5m)). This amounts to £5.6m each year.

But the amount being paid in the next year is £8m and so the company should debit a prepayment (credit pension costs) with (8 − 5.6) £2.4m.

During the following 3 years, payments will be £6m each year. This involves making further prepayments of (6 − 5.6) £0.4m each year. By the end of the 4th year, total prepayments will be £3.6m − i.e. (1 × 2.4) + (3 × 0.4).

During the next 6 years, contributions will be £5m each year. In order to increase these to the required cost of £5.6m per year, an amount will be debited to pension costs (credited to prepayments) of £0.6m each year. The prepayment of £3.6m will therefore be eliminated (6 × £0.6) by the end of the 10th year.

Notes

Improving examination performance on SSAPs

Most students have access to something which is usually called 'examination technique' and there would be no point in repeating all the valuable advice which is given under that heading. There are, however, some points which are particularly important when it comes to answering questions on SSAPs.

Probably (remember the word probably!) the most important point is the degree of caution needed in the answer. I have lost count of the number of times I find a student's answer starting off with something like '. . . this is most definitely an adjusting event because. . .', yet when I look at the question I find the examiner has couched it in such deliberately vague terms he was obviously hoping to evoke a wider discussion. Accountancy students, however, seem to think that they must give definite answers rather than explore all the possibilities. Perhaps that attitude is related to our fascination over the symmetry of the double entry equation.

Here are some words which you should treat as part of your armoury: it appears; seems to indicate; might suggest; seems to imply; may be; perhaps; probably; further enquiry; prima facie (I like that one, it sounds authoritative). Having made the point I am sure you can probably (!) dream up others.

You should not take it too far otherwise your answer might become so concealed in a mist of vagueness as to appear like waffle.

If you would like to refer to some examples of how to explore items that appear to be definite you should look back to the comments made in some of the illustrations in this guide, like SSAPs 13 and SSAP 17.

A further point which may be of help is to make use of the thinking tools developed by Edward de Bono and published by Direct Education Services in 1973. The two tools which should help students with their answers on SSAPs are PMI and CAF.

PMI stands for plus points, minus points, and interesting points. It becomes a tool because it has been given the name PMI. It is one of the most helpful tools to use with many questions which end in the command: 'discuss' because it will stop you from reacting in an emotional way to your own bias and preferences. It will force you into making a critical examination of many more points than you would normally do without the tool.

CAF stands for 'consider all factors' and it is particularly relevant to many questions on SSAPs because of the way they interact with other SSAPs and also with various pieces of legislation. Furthermore there are many factors in any one SSAP which could be relevant to the question. Without the tool there is a danger of limiting your answer to one narrow angle. By taking it into the exam room you will be forced to think more widely.

Hopefully, the way in which SSAPs have been analysed throughout this guide will provide a pattern which can be used alongside the tool of CAF.

Exams are a crisis point and it those who manage to deal with crisis best who make the grade. There's nothing wrong with having a few tools other than your calculator to help you through the crisis. Good luck.

Appendix 1
Examples from published accounts

The following examples either relate to some of the later SSAPs which are in their early days of application or they contain something controversial which readers might like to use as a basis for further exploration.

1) SSAP 6 12 and 19, treatment of surplus on sale of property.

(a) Trusthouse Forte plc, 31 October 1984. Extract from accounting policy note:

Properties: Freehold and long leasehold properties are revalued at intervals of not more than seven years and the resultant valuation is included in the balance sheet unless the surplus or deficit is immaterial. Short leaseholds are included in the balance sheet at cost or revaluation prior to 31st October, 1978, plus subsequent additions at cost or valuation at the date of acquisition.

Where the group disposes of properties in the normal course of trading, the profit or loss arising is included in trading profit. The profit or loss represents the difference between the net proceeds of sale and and historical cost.

(b) The Rank Organisation, 31 October 1984. Extract from accounting policy note:

Depreciation of fixed assets. Properties held for investment.

Completed investment properties are revalued regularly and reflected in the investment property revaluation reserve. Profits or losses on disposal are dealt with in extraordinary items and are arrived at by comparing sale proceeds with the revalued book amount at the beginning of the year and making an appropriate transfer from revaluation reserve of the previously unrealized surplus or deficit relating thereto which has become realized as a result of the disposal, to arrive at the realized profit or loss against historical cost.

(*Comment*: The revised SSAP 6, August 1986, would probably rule against these items being treated as extraordinary but the basis used to calculate the gain or loss on disposal has not been resolved: see SSAP 12 in the guide.)

2) SSAP 20. Gains and losses on translation. Reserve movement dealt with on retained earnings, also departure from Companies Act.

(a) Christies International plc, 31 December 1983. Note 27 Profit and loss account:

In order to comply with Statement of Accounting Practice No. 20 there has been a departure from the accounting principles of Schedule 8 of the Companies Act 1948 (*now Sch. 4 CA 1985*) by inclusion in the profit and loss account balance of unrealized translation gains arising on the translation of the share capital and distributable reserves of the Group's overseas subsidiary Companies. The gains arising during 1983 amounted to £666,000 (1982 £930,000).

(b) Bass plc, 30 September 1984. Extract from accounting policy note:

Assets and liabilities in foreign currencies together with the trading results of overseas subsidiaries are translated into sterling at the relevant rates of exchange ruling at the balance sheet date. Exchange differences whether realized or unrealized:

i) on overseas net assets are taken to retained earnings.

ii) on foreign currency borrowings of the investing company are taken to retained earnings to the extent that these differences match those in (i) above but are included as part of cost of borrowing where these differences are unmatched.

All other exchange differences are dealt with in arriving at the trading profit.

The company's investment in overseas subsidiaries is translated into sterling at the rate of exchange ruling at the date of acquisition.

Extract from disclosure in Note 17 Reserves:

	Group £m	*Company* £m
b) Profit and loss account		
Retained earnings at 30 September 1983	731.7	219.2
Exchange adjustment on revaluation reserves (17a)	(.4)	—
Exchange adjustment on assets, less borrowings	.3	—
Revaluation element in depreciation charge (17a)	1.4	—
Premium on acquisition of subsidiaries	(1.3)	—
Retained earnings for the year	91.4	5.8
Retained earnings at 30 September 1984	823.1	225.0

The amount of exchange losses on foreign currency borrowings offset above using the matching concept is	4.3

3) SSAP 22, Goodwill

British Petroleum Company plc, 31 December 1984. Extract from accounting policy note

GOODWILL

Goodwill is the excess of purchase consideration over the fair value of net assets acquired. It is capitalized and amortized over its estimated useful economic life, limited to a maximum period of five years.

4) SSAP 21, Finance leases, capitalization of leased assets and related obligations:

The Caledonian Aviation Group plc, 31 October 1984. Extract from accounting policy note:

Accounting for Tangible Fixed Assets.

Expenditure on tangible fixed assets, including those subject to hire purchase arrangements, is capitalized.

Tangible fixed assets operated under terms of finance leases are also capitalised at a value equal to the cost incurred by the lessor in acquiring the relevant assets and depreciated in the same manner as owned assets. Leases are regarded as finance leases where their terms transfer to the lessee substantially all the benefits and burdens of ownership other than the right to title. The capital element of future lease payments is included under loans and term finance.

Extracts from other notes to the accounts include the following:

9)   Tangible fixed assets

	Aircraft fleet	
	Owned	*Leased*
	£'000	£'000
Cost or valuation 1st November, 1983	88,511	109,441
Foreign exchange adjustments	3,458	12,625

17)   Loans and Term Finance

	Group	*Company*
	£'000	£'000
Term Finance – Wholly repayable within five years: Hire purchase arrangements – Sterling	1,877	—
Term Finance – U.S. Dollars	17,509	—

Appendix 2
Harmonization of international and UK standards

International standards are issued by the International Accounting Standards Committee (IASC) which was formed in 1973. It came into being as a result of an agreement between the main accountancy bodies in several of the more developed countries. It seeks to formulate and publish standards and to promote their acceptance and observation on a worldwide basis. Its members agreed to use their best endeavours to ensure that published accounts comply with international standards.

International standards are not directly applicable to UK. The ASC supports the work of the IASC and as far as possible seeks to incorporate the provisions of international standards into our own domestic standards. SSAPs must also be applied to financial statements of an overseas entity if the results of that entity are to incorporated into those of a UK group. Neither the IASC nor the accountancy profession has the power to enforce compliance with International Standards. The work of the IASC is therefore seen as one of persuasion and its success depends on the recognition of its work by interested parties in each country.

The IASC concentrates on essentials and endeavours not to make IASs so complex that they could not be applied effectively on a worldwide basis. Students of accountancy are well advised to read the international standards even if they do not form part of their examinable syllabus. The language used is clearer than many SSAPs and this sometimes helps to make sense of what might otherwise seem to be a complex point.

The following table sets out the current position regarding harmonization of international standards with SSAPs. In some cases the subject of one SSAP is dealt with by two IASs and in some cases the reverse applies:

	SSAP	IAS
Associated companies	1	3
Disclosure of accounting policies	2	1
Earnings per share	3	none
Government grants	4	20
Value added tax	5	none

Extraordinary items and prior year adjustments	6	8
Taxation under the imputation system	8	none
Stocks and work in progress, including long-term contracts	9	2 and 11
Source and application of funds	10	7
Depreciation	12	4
Research and development	13	9
Group accounts	14	3
Deferred taxation	15	12
Current cost accounting	16	15
Post balance sheet events	17	10
Contingencies	18	10
Investment properties	19	none
Foreign currency translation	20	21
Leases and hire purchase contracts	21	17
Goodwill	22	22
Acquisitions and mergers	23	22
Accounting for pension costs	24	19

The following IASs have not yet been incorporated into SSAPs:

IAS 5 Information to be disclosed in financial statements
IAS 13 Presentation of current assets and current liabilities
IAS 14 Reporting financial information by segment
IAS 16 Accounting for property plant and equipment
IAS 18 Revenue recognition
IAS 23 Capitalization of borrowing costs
IAS 24 Related party disclosures
IAS 25 Accounting for investments
IAS 26 Accounting and reporting by retirement benefit plans

IASs 5 13 and 16 are to a large extent covered by the accounting requirements of the 1985 Companies Act and the Stock exchange requirements for listed companies. IAS 18 reflects the generally accepted practices in UK and does not appear to call for a domestic standard to be issued. The subject of IAS 26 is to a large extent covered by the legal accounting requirements in The Social Security Act 1985 and is supported by SORP 1. IAS 14 is under discussion through ED45, and IAS 24 is the subject of ED46.

Appendix 3
A summary of the latest debate on inflation accounting

Historic cost accounting is sometimes criticised in the sense that balance sheet values are residual figures, arising after the measurement of profit. Economists and accounting academics often argue that profit should be a residual figure derived from a measurement of the increase in net worth. Accountants have not yet defined profit and there is a tendency for them to see it in terms of a transaction matching process.

Capital maintenance

The quotation most frequently referred to when searching for a definition of profit, is a statement made in 1939 by an economist, Sir John Hicks, as follows:

> The purpose of income calculations is to give people an indication of the amount they can consume without impoverishing themselves.

This could be applied to accounting profit in terms such as: 'the maximum value which could be distributed and leave the business as well off at the end of the year as it was at the beginning.' The difficulty is how to define 'well offness' which, in accounting terminology, refers to the capital. Capital may be viewed from inside the company and thought of as a sum represented by the net operating assets, or viewed externally as a sum of financial capital attributable to the shareholders.

This problem was given some official publicity through a statement in the explanatory notes to SSAP 16 which stated that: 'In most systems of accounting, profit is determined after making charges against revenue to provide for the maintenance of capital. Since the definition of capital varies according to the accounting concept adopted, the method of determining profit also varies.'

The various concepts of capital were not discussed in SSAP 16 but they are dealt with in the ASC's Handbook on 'Accounting for the effects of changing prices' which was issued when SSAP 16 was finally withdrawn.

In general terms, this concept of profit measurement is referred to as the 'capital maintenance concept' and most of the discussion centres around the various ways in which capital can be measured. The three popular concepts of capital, together with their effect on accounting measurements, are as follows:

Historical cost: capital is the shareholders funds, represented by the net assets which are measured by using the value of money at the time of the transaction.

Current revenues are matched with costs which, in many cases, were incurred at an earlier time. Where these charges relate to the consumption of assets (e.g. stock and fixed assets) there will be no charge against revenue for the increased cost of replacing the asset consumed. A full distribution of profit measured on this basis could result in the distribution of sums needed to maintain the operating capital.

Balance sheet values are unrealistic and give a distorted view of resources employed in the business. Calculations of the return on capital employed are misleading since, in real terms, they tend to be based on overstated profit and understated net assets.

Current cost: net assets are measured in terms of their value to the business. In the case of non-monetary assets this is based, roughly speaking, on replacement costs.

Generally speaking, SSAP 16 provided that replacement costs could be determined by the use of indices for the specific class of physical asset

Charges against revenue for assets consumed in earning that revenue are measured in terms of their value to the business (e.g. replacement cost) at the time consumed. A full distribution of profit measured on this basis should leave the business with the same level of operating assets as it had at the beginning of the period.

In some versions of CCA (e.g. the SSAP 16 version) there is a further charge against revenue to recognise the additional finance needed to replace stocks if input prices rise between the time of sale and the time cash is received from debtors. The compensating effect which arises through the use of trade credit for purchases is also recognised. The adjustment to profit was referred to as the Monetary Working Capital Adjustment (MWCA) and was based (roughly) on debtors less creditors.

Operating results and balance sheet values under CCA are more realistic but they are not directly comparable with those for earlier years since no attempt is made to restate values in terms of a constant unit of measurement.

Constant purchasing power: all items in the accounts are expressed in terms of a constant purchasing power unit. Non-monetary assets are revalued according to changes in the general purchasing power of money since their acquisition (usually based on changes in the the Retail Price Index). Profit can then be related to an increase in capital over the period (as measured by these units) after making allowances for any capital injections and distributions.

Various methods of using purchasing power units as a way of making accounting measurements have been developed. Where these units are based on the purchasing power of money at the reporting date, the system is known as 'current purchasing power' accounting.

The objective of the system is to maintain the shareholders' financial capital in terms of its purchasing power. The operating capital of the business will not be maintained unless rates of inflation being experienced by the company (on its various inputs) equate with the general rate of inflation as measured by the RPI.

Since all figures are converted into a constant unit (the purchasing power unit) the comparison of results over a period of years will be more meaningful – like is being compared with like. It would be difficult to make comparisons with other companies where they had a different accounting date.

The real terms system – ASC handbook

The two concepts of capital maintenance covered by the previous notes are as follows:

1) the operating capital maintenance concept which forms the basis of current cost accounting and deals with the impact of inflation on internal operations of the business; and
2) the financial capital maintenance concept which looks at capital from the shareholders point of view and measures it either in nominal pounds (HCA) or in terms of purchasing power units (CPP).

The 'real terms system' is a hybrid between CCA and CPP. The basic approach is as follows:

(a) Calculate capital at the beginning of the period based on current cost asset values at that time.
(b) Restate this figure into what it would be in terms of purchasing power units at the reporting date. In other words, convert it into current pounds by making adjustments for the general rate of inflation over the period.
(c) Compare the figure in (b), with capital at the end of the year based on current cost asset values. Profit (or loss) is the difference between the two after making adjustments for any distributions and/or capital introduced during the period.

This method attempts to maintain financial capital in real terms.

Conclusion

Despite its limitations, historical cost accounting continues to be the universally preferred method of financial reporting by business enterprises. It forms the basis of legal accounts throughout the European Community.

The practice of modifying historical cost accounts by the revaluation of certain assets is not considered adequate since revaluations tend to be infrequent and limited to certain types of long-term asset.

It is sometimes argued that historical cost accounts are adequate for stewardship purposes but not for decision making, particularly on matters such as dividend payments, and for investment and financing decisions. One interesting set of statistics in the ASC's Handbook compares dividend payments with both historic and current cost profits for a sample of public companies over the years 1980 to 1984. In 1982 dividends were less than 50% of historic cost profits but were 130% of current cost profits!

The accounting profession has been unable to agree on any definitive method for inflation accounting and the ASC's latest initiative is to make recommendations through the Handbook. Their recommended method is to publish supplementary figures based on current cost, using either the operating or financial capital maintenance concepts.

Illustrations   HCA, CCA, CPP, and real terms

The opening balance sheet of a business is as follows:

Cash at bank	1 000
Stock (1 item)	1 000
	2 000
Capital and reserves	2 000

Transactions during the period (all for cash) were as follows:

Opening stock item sold for	1 500
Replaced at a cost of	1 200
Expenses paid	300

Index information:

	RPI	Stock
At start of period	100	100
On sale and replacement of stock	110	120
At end of period	120	130

1)   Historical cost accounts:

Profit and loss account

Sales	1 500
Cost of sales	1 000
Gross profit	500
Expenses	300
Net profit	200

Balance sheet

Cash at bank	1 000
Stock (1 item)	1 200
	2 200
Capital and reserves	
Brought forward	2 000
Net profit for period	200
	2 200

Note: The opening financial capital as measured in nominal pounds of £2,000 has been maintained, allowing a surplus of £200 to be recognized. But there has been no real increase in the level of operating assets.

2) Current cost accounts:

Profit and loss account		Balance sheet		
Sales	1 500	Cash at bank		1 000
Cost of sales	1 200	Stock (1 item)		
Gross profit	300	(1 200 × 130/120)		1 300
Expenses	300			2 300
Net profit	nil	Capital and reserves		
		Brought forward		2 000
		Net profit for period		nil
		Current cost reserve		
		Realized holding gain	200	
		Unrealized holding gain	100	300
				2 300

Note: The operating capital must be maintained before any surplus is recognized. Since there has been no increase in the level of operating assets, there is no operating gain.

3) Current purchasing power accounts:

Profit and loss account			Balance sheet		
Sales		1 636	Cash at bank		1 000
(1 500 × 120/110)			Stock		1 309
Cost of sales:					2 309
Opening stock	1 200				
(1 000 × 120/100)					
Purchases	1 309		Capital and		
(1 200 × 120/110)			reserves		
	2 509		Brought forward		2 400
Closing stock	1 309		(2 000 × 120/100)		
(1 200 × 120/110)		1 200	Net loss		(91)
Gross profit		436			2 309
Expenses		327			
(300 × 120/110)					
		109			
Loss on holding monetary items					
Opening balance	200				
(1 000 × 20/100)					
Net receipts	0	200			
(0 × 10/100)					
Net loss		(91)			

Note: The financial capital measured in terms of its purchasing power must be maintained before any surplus is recognized. With 20% inflation, the purchasing power of the opening capital of £2,000 is represented by £2,400 at the accounting date, yet assets (measured in year end CPP units) are only £2,309. Thus a loss of £91 (2,400 − 2,309) has to be recognized.

4) Real terms accounting:
The profit is calculated as follows:

CCA value at start	2 000
Adjusted to year end purchasing power units	2 400
CCA value at end	2 300
Loss	(100)

Basic profit and loss account

HCA profit		200
Add unrealized holding gains arising during the year	100	
Less inflation adjustment to shareholder's funds	400	300
		—
Loss		(100)

Balance sheet

Cash at bank	1 000
Stock (CCA)	1 300
	2 300
Capital and reserves	
Brought forward	2 000
Financial maintenance reserve	400
Loss for year	(100)
	2 300

Note: In this case, the amount required to maintain financial capital in terms of its purchasing power has been recognized, but non-monetary assets in the closing balance sheet are shown at current cost.

Notes

Index

In order to reduce the number of reference points, the following index does not include page numbers for parallel topics included in the SSAP overview.